G000069110

WHERE THE WORLD MEETS TO PRAY

Daniele Och
UK editor

INVITATIONAL

INTERDENOMINATIONAL

INTERNATIONAL

37 LANGUAGES

Multiple formats are available in some languages

15 The Chambers, Vineyard
Abingdon OX14 3FE
brf.org.uk

Bible Reading Fellowship is a charity (233280)
and company limited by guarantee (301324),
registered in England and Wales

ISBN 978 1 80039 137 6

Originally published in the USA by The Upper Room® upperroom.org
US edition © 2021 The Upper Room, Nashville, TN (USA). All rights reserved.
This edition © Bible Reading Fellowship 2021
Cover image © Martin Beek

Acknowledgements

Scripture quotations marked with the following abbreviations are taken from the
version shown. Where no acronym is given, the quotation is taken from the same
version as the headline reference.

NTE: *The New Testament for Everyone* copyright © Nicholas Thomas Wright 2011.

NIV: The Holy Bible, New International Version (Anglicised edition) copyright © 1979,
1984, 2011 by Biblica. Used by permission of Hodder & Stoughton Publishers, an
Hachette UK company. All rights reserved. 'NIV' is a registered trademark of Biblica.
UK trademark number 1448790.

NRSV: The New Revised Standard Version of the Bible, Anglicised Edition, copyright
© 1989, 1995 by the Division of Christian Education of the National Council of the
Churches of Christ in the USA. Used by permission. All rights reserved.

CEB: copyright © 2011 by Common English Bible.

KJV: the Authorised Version of the Bible (The King James Bible), the rights in which
are vested in the Crown, are reproduced by permission of the Crown's Patentee,
Cambridge University Press.

GNT: the Good News Bible published by The Bible Societies/HarperCollins
Publishers Ltd, UK © American Bible Society 1966, 1971, 1976, 1992, used with
permission.

A catalogue record for this book is available from the British Library

Printed by Gutenberg Press, Tarxien, Malta

How to use *The Upper Room*

The Upper Room is ideal in helping us spend a quiet time with God each day. Each daily entry is based on a passage of scripture and is followed by a meditation and prayer. Each person who contributes a meditation to the magazine seeks to relate their experience of God in a way that will help those who use *The Upper Room* every day.

Here are some guidelines to help you make best use of *The Upper Room*:

1 Read the passage of scripture. It is a good idea to read it more than once, in order to have a fuller understanding of what it is about and what you can learn from it.
2 Read the meditation. How does it relate to your own experience? Can you identify with what the writer has outlined from their own experience or understanding?
3 Pray the written prayer. Think about how you can use it to relate to people you know or situations that need your prayers today.
4 Think about the contributor who has written the meditation. Some users of the *The Upper Room* include this person in their prayers for the day.
5 Meditate on the 'Thought for the day' and the 'Prayer focus', perhaps using them again as the focus for prayer or direction for action.

Why is it important to have a daily quiet time? Many people will agree that it is the best way of keeping in touch every day with the God who sustains us and who sends us out to do his will and show his love to the people we encounter each day. Meeting with God in this way reassures us of his presence with us, helps us to discern his will for us and makes us part of his worldwide family of Christian people through our prayers.

I hope that you will be encouraged as you use the magazine regularly as part of your daily devotions, and that God will richly bless you as you read his word and seek to learn more about him.

Daniele Och
UK editor

Could you write a meditation for *The Upper Room*?

The Upper Room is, as far as we know, unique in that its readers are its writers. Known as the place 'where the world meets to pray', contributors from the widest imaginable range of backgrounds and locations share their faith experiences and biblical insights with the entire *Upper Room* community.

BRF publishes the UK edition of *The Upper Room*, and editor Daniele Och is on the lookout for some new UK-based writers. So, if you think you could write a short meditation on a Bible verse, rooted in your own experience, why not have a go? The aim of each day's meditation is to help people make a connection between their lives and what God is doing in the world, but to have any chance of being published, it's important to write in an appropriate style. You need to include:

1   a Bible reading and quotation
2   the meditation (200–250 words)
3   a short prayer
4   a Thought for the day
5   a Prayer focus

The maximum word count for all these elements together is 300. Send your reflection by email to **Upper.Room@brf.org.uk** or by post to **The Upper Room, BRF, 15 The Chambers, Vineyard, Abingdon, Oxford OX14 3FE**. Make sure your name and contact details are clear. Only successful contributors will be contacted and no correspondence will be entered into. A modest fee is paid for successful submissions.

Top tips for writing for *The Upper Room*

*   Begin by studying and meditating on the Bible, so that its power supports your words.
*   Connect scripture with your own life. Your experience is unique.
*   Make only one point.
*   Avoid using very familiar illustrations – try to be original.
*   Avoid the use of 'You should…', 'You need to…', 'You must…'
*   Use language and examples that appeal to the senses.
*   Indicate which Bible version you use for quotations.
*   Remember your audience.

Good luck! We look forward to reading your meditation.

Lifting up Jesus

Just as Moses lifted up the snake in the desert, in the same way the son of man must be lifted up, so that everyone who believes in him may share in the life of God's new age. This, you see, is how much God loved the world: enough to give his only, special son, so that everyone who believes in him should not be lost but should share in the life of God's new age.

John 3:14–16 (NTE)

As we begin a new year it can be helpful to pause and refresh ourselves on the basics of our Christian faith. At its core, the good news of Jesus is that he is the new Moses who leads us out of exile into the 'life of God's new age'. Jesus is also the 'once for all' sacrifice (Hebrews 10:10), suffering servant (Isaiah 52:13) and lamb that has been lifted up and is now seated in the throne of God (Revelation 7:17). Jesus is the living embodiment of hope and healing for the broken human family.

In a world that needs tangible reminders of God's love, let us be bold in demonstrating the love modelled by Jesus, who was willing to be lifted up, broken and poured out for the restoration of the world. Remember, he even gave his life for those who betrayed him. The hardest commands of Jesus to put into practice are those that call us to love our neighbour, to love our enemies and to love ourselves (Luke 10:27). This year, may we call upon the Holy Spirit to give us eyes to see others and ourselves as God sees us: worthy of transformational grace and love because of Jesus' ongoing, shepherding intercession for us.

Revd Kimberly Orr
World editor and publisher

Portuguese-Africa edition

French edition

Kiswahili edition

Writers featured in this issue of *The Upper Room*:

Muyiwa Olaiya (Nigeria) • Valerie Clark (South Africa)
• Raphael Williams (South Africa) • Rafiki Heed (Tanzania)
• Vimbai Chizarura (Zimbabwe)

Gifts to the international
editions of *The Upper Room*
help the world meet to pray.
upperroom.org/gift

The editor writes...

Your word is a lamp for my feet, a light on my path.
Psalm 119:105 (NIV)

Happy new year! The year 2022 is a significant one for BRF. One hundred years ago, in a church in south London, The Fellowship of St Matthew was begun in response to a congregation's eagerness for informed and helpful support in building a habit of daily Bible reading. In 1926, it became known as the Bible Reading Fellowship (BRF) as its influence spread and more church communities subscribed to the notes and prayers which were offered. Today, BRF resources people and groups as they grow in faith, encouraging them to deepen their relationship with God and to share the good news of Jesus Christ with others. While the work of BRF takes many forms, at the heart of it still is to encourage regular, reflective reading of scripture.

Careful, attentive reading of the Bible is the theme of several meditations in this issue of *The Upper Room* (see, for example, 15, 16, 18 March; 17, 23 April). Recently, I was watching a video in which a film enthusiast was explaining his favourite scene in a famous movie. Although the segment in question was less than 20 seconds, by watching it slowly and repeatedly and focusing on the details of the acting, direction, cinematography and editing, the critic was able to show how, in such a short space of time, a great deal of meaning was conveyed.

I have found that a similar approach to Bible reading has been extremely helpful. That is, reading and rereading a passage carefully and prayerfully, paying attention to its context (both within the Bible itself and the wider historical context), and hearing the perspectives of others have been a great benefit to me in understanding the Bible, and most importantly to therefore learn more about who God is, what he is like and what he is saying to me.

In presenting you with this issue of *The Upper Room*, gathering reflections from its worldwide community of readers, we at BRF hope that you too may deepen your relationship with God by reading and reflecting upon his word.

Daniele Och
UK editor

PS – I am delighted to include in this issue the meditations by the two runners-up of BRF's *The Upper Room* writing competition 2020, Clare O'Driscoll and Valerie Eker. You can read them on 4 February and 22 February.

Counting the days

Read Psalm 90:1–12

Teach us to number our days, that we may gain a heart of wisdom.
Psalm 90:12 (NIV)

This year I resolved not to forget what day it is. I know it sounds a bit absurd to forget what day it is, but sometimes it happens. In high school we were instructed to write the date on each page in our notebook. At university, this practice was not required, making it easier to lose track of the days.

Today's reading reminds us to think about how we spend our days. Do we pass our time not even knowing what day it is? Or do we strive to live life to the fullest according to God's will, gaining insight and praising God? Today is a good day to begin to live a purpose-filled life guided by the Holy Spirit. Now, using a pocket calendar, I have found a tool that helps me set and remember my agenda for the day. Each day lived for God is significant; it offers a new opportunity to bless the Lord and bless others, and ask God to 'teach us to number our days' and increase our knowledge.

Prayer: *Giver of life, each day is a gift from you. Help us to acknowledge that gift as we work to do your will and praise your name. Amen*

Thought for the day: My agenda today is to be grateful for God's blessings.

Frine Paola Cedano Berroa (Dominican Republic)

Recognition

Read John 13:31–35

'Just as I have loved you, you also should love one another. By this everyone will know that you are my disciples, if you have love for one another.'
John 13:34–35 (NRSV)

When I was younger, my grandparents adopted me after my mother died. My grandmother was my biggest fan and supported me in school and in my extracurricular activities. She truly loved me. We were always together, so people would always associate me with her and her with me. When we were apart, people would always ask about the other person.

Since then, I have made poor choices and am now in prison. My grandmother passed away a couple of years ago. Since I don't get visits, I have a job as the visitation park photographer. Now, when families come for visits, I recognise them and associate them with the person they are visiting. Sometimes, even when I have not met someone's family before, I recognise similar features and I end up seeing that person in them.

I wonder if people recognise us as always being with God. When they see us, do they also see God and recognise Christ in us? Scripture reminds us that others will see Christ in us when we love one another.

Prayer: *Dear Jesus, help us to reflect you in all that we do. May others see you in us today and every day. Amen*

Thought for the day: Does my relationship with Jesus show through my actions?

Nicholas Patterson (Florida, USA)

A heart of love

Read Ephesians 3:14–21

I pray that you, being rooted and established in love, may have power… to grasp how wide and long and high and deep is the love of Christ, and to know this love that surpasses knowledge – that you may be filled to the measure of all the fullness of God.
Ephesians 3:17–19 (NIV)

One morning the Holy Spirit taught me a lesson about the love of Christ through my son Melvin. Melvin has autism. He is 44 years old now, and what a journey we have had!

Two weeks ago Melvin said to me, 'I would like to talk with my dad before he dies.' Stunned by his request, I didn't know how to reply. His dad had never accepted him, and in his disappointment had withdrawn himself from Melvin. Though Melvin has not seen his dad for many years, he loves him. His heart remembers his dad, and he wants to see him.

Others may turn their backs on us, but Christ turns towards us with love. We may forget Christ, but Christ remembers us. When we are lost, Christ finds us. When we are in trouble, Christ rescues us.

This steadfast love is what the apostle Paul, in the verse quoted above, prayed for us to know – a love that can fill us with all the fullness of God!

Prayer: *Dear loving Father, teach our hearts to know the unconditional love of Christ Jesus and to let that love overflow towards others. Amen*

Thought for the day: Christ's love for me knows no bounds.

Bernadette Butler (Ohio, USA)

Holding on to God

Read Job 1:13–22

In all this, Job did not sin by charging God with wrongdoing.
Job 1:22 (NIV)

This year I have suffered heavily from anxiety and depression. I never knew how debilitating mental illness could be. My brain and body seemed to stop functioning. I had ceased my regular morning prayer routine and suffered from a sense of God's absence.

Part of living is undergoing such trying times. We don't want them, but they hit us at the most unexpected moments. It can be easy to respond like Job's friends and explain them away.

Like Job, we wrestle with these experiences and wonder why this is happening to us. I have concluded that they just *are*. They are not the revenge of God or punishment for our sinfulness or random attacks of a meaningless universe. They are dark nights that show up on bright days. And somehow we find that God was always there in the midst of it.

When we experience difficulties, we can remember Job, who discovered that, no matter what, God *is*. God is beyond all time, the creator and loving sustainer of all of life. So when we experience the darkness of illness – mental or otherwise – we can sit with two truths: challenges just *are*, and God *is*. That knowledge can give us hope to hold on.

Prayer: *Loving God, hold us in your embrace when we are struggling to hold on to you and to a joyful life. Amen*

Thought for the day: Because God loves me, I can hold on.

Ted Witham (Western Australia, Australia)

Praise prayers

Read Psalm 33:1–9

Sing to the Lord a new song! Sing his praise from the ends of the earth!

Isaiah 42:10 (CEB)

One day I began my usual morning prayers. I prayed for my children's needs, my needs and the needs of friends and family. Suddenly, a vivid image of a gumball machine popped into my head. As a child, I enjoyed putting a coin in the slot, turning the handle and having a colourful gumball fall into my hand. I realised I had been praying as if I were inserting coins into a gumball machine. Almost all of my prayers were petitions, and I was acting as though I expected God's answers to drop into my life like gumballs into my hand. While God is compassionate and willing to help us when we ask, I realised I was taking for granted the wonders of creation, God's generous gifts and the sacrifice Christ made for us.

Now when I pray, I begin with praise. Instead of immediately thinking of what may be lacking in my life and the lives of my loved ones, I find joy in first recognising the amazing love and generosity of God. And I find that when my 'praise prayers' remind me of all that God has done, my 'please prayers' come from a trusting, thankful heart.

Prayer: *Dear Lord God, help us not to wait until we need something, but to stay close to you at all times, expressing praise and trust. Amen*

Thought for the day: I will balance my prayerful petitions with praise for what God has done.

Valerie Bryant Bennett (Tennessee, USA)

Day of the Kings

Read Matthew 2:1–12

On coming to the house, they saw the child with his mother Mary, and they bowed down and worshipped him.

Matthew 2:11 (NIV)

On 6 January of each year, many of my neighbours across the border in Mexico celebrate Día de los Reyes (Day of the Kings). This holiday is a celebration of the faithfulness of the magi and of the generous gifts they brought to the Christ child.

But who were these magi who were searching for the king of the Jews? Were they really kings or royalty from other kingdoms? Were they astrologers or nomads? Were there only three? Did they travel with a caravan for safety? And why is it that Matthew is the only one of the gospels to tell this story of faith and hope?

What is clear to me is the deep faith of the magi, who were willing to leave their homes and travel far, believing the truth of a prophecy and following a moving star. When the star finally led them to Bethlehem, they humbly presented their gifts and worshipped the child, the promised Messiah.

So whether we celebrate 6 January as the ending of the twelve days of Christmas, or in recognition of the journey of the magi, or as Epiphany – the revealing of Christ's birth to the world – it is a special time to celebrate faith, love and hope in the promises of God.

Prayer: *Heavenly Father, thank you for the gift the magi gave to us – their story of faith. Give us faith so that we also are willing to journey into the unknown to seek our Saviour. In his name we pray. Amen*

Thought for the day: Today I will be bold in seeking Christ Jesus.

Douglas Wingert (Arizona, USA)

Not alone

Read 1 Kings 19:9–18

'I have told you these things, so that in me you may have peace. In this world you will have trouble. But take heart! I have overcome the world.'
John 16:33 (NIV)

For followers of Christ, it can be lonely in the workplace, school playground, university campus, neighbourhood group or even in our family. When conversations feel unedifying or ungodly and we don't want to laugh at rude jokes or join in gossip, we may feel like outsiders who don't belong.

We see throughout the Bible that declaring our faith can lead to persecution or ridicule. For instance, Elijah felt this way when he stood against the wicked prophets of Baal. Once he defeated them, he was threatened by Queen Jezebel and fled into the wilderness. There, Elijah confessed to God that he felt alone in his stand for what was right. God reminded him that there were others who were loyal believers. He was not alone.

Jesus also told his followers that they would have times of loneliness, but he promised that he would never leave or forsake them. The same is true for us. We may have trouble in this world, but we can take courage because Jesus has overcome the world. Christ is with us whatever our circumstances.

Prayer: *Dear Lord, help us to remember your presence when we feel alone. We pray the prayer Jesus taught us, 'Father, hallowed be your name, your kingdom come. Give us each day our daily bread. Forgive us our sins, for we also forgive everyone who sins against us. And lead us not into temptation.'* Amen*

Thought for the day: I can have courage because God is with me.

Valerie Clark (KwaZulu-Natal, South Africa)

Behind the scenes

Read John 6:5–13

Andrew… spoke up, 'Here is a boy with five small barley loaves and two small fish, but how far will they go among so many?'
John 6:8–9 (NIV)

The account of the boy who gave up his lunch to feed the multitudes is a familiar one. But I often wonder about the one who prepared the boy's lunch.

When he saw the great crowd waiting for him, Jesus tested Philip by asking where they were to find food for the people to eat. Philip said it would take more than eight months' wages to buy food for 5.000 men, not to mention the women and children.

Andrew found a boy who had brought lunch, but he asked, 'How far will they go among so many?' Yet, in the hands of Jesus, those five small loaves and two small fish fed the multitudes with twelve baskets left over.

I imagine the boy's mother making his lunch at home, lovingly shaping and baking the small loaves, and placing the fish into a small sack. I imagine her faithfully preparing her son for the day, not knowing he would be a part of an encounter with the miracle-working Saviour.

When I wonder if what I do for Jesus has value, I think of the people who provided the raw materials for a miracle that day. My behind-the-scenes faithfulness can be part of creative miracles in the hands of Jesus.

Prayer: *Dear Lord, magnify our small, faithful efforts so that we may join you in blessing others today. Amen*

Thought for the day: Even humble efforts can change lives.

Inger J. Logelin (Washington, USA)

Continued growth

Read Ephesians 4:25–32

Be kind, compassionate, and forgiving to each other, in the same way God forgave you in Christ.
Ephesians 4:32 (CEB)

My little farming homestead is nestled in a suburban, woodsy neighbourhood. In the late afternoon, I love to walk through the trees behind the house as the light dances among the leaves. Sometimes, I lie down on the ground and look up in awe at the formidable old oaks and tulip poplars. If I catch the light just right, however, I can also see scars or bumps on the outside of a tree – a place where the bark is clearly not unified with the rest of the trunk. Yet the tree continues to grow past the scars and live a healthy life.

In our scripture today, we learn that the same can be said about the process of forgiveness. Forgiveness is not just about letting go; it's also about moving forward – not holding someone else or ourselves captive to the hurts of the past. It's about being actively compassionate and offering words and acts of grace, just as God has done for us through Jesus Christ.

Like the trees, we have wounds; but we do not have to become stunted by them. Through lives of prayer and acts of forgiveness, we allow God to heal our scars, create new life and guide us in our continued growth.

Prayer: *Gracious creator, despite our sadness and pain, help us dare to live with compassion. Heal our wounds so that we may embrace new life. Amen*

Thought for the day: Compassionate forgiveness is a part of my journey towards wholeness.

Cameron Kempson (North Carolina, USA)

God's beloved

Read Psalm 139:13–18
'How can you believe since you accept glory from one another but do not seek the glory that comes from the only God?'
John 5:44 (NIV)

My family and I are serving as missionaries in Tanzania, Africa. I accompany my daughter Olivia to school in a *bajaji* (a three-wheeled tut-tut taxi). Most days, the drivers are quiet or make small talk. But one day a driver berated Olivia for having substandard Swahili. He barked at me for not teaching her better.

We dropped Olivia off at school. Later, I told her, 'I'm sorry that the driver was so mean to you.' She looked at me in confusion. Mean to her? She hadn't even noticed. I was amazed. Perhaps she felt safe enough in my presence that any criticism or accusation did not affect her.

Oh, how I want that assurance! I want to walk through life confident that my divine parent is in charge and knowing that criticism won't matter because I rest in God's truths.

In John 5:44 Jesus gets to the heart of the issue. It is our creator who determines our identity, not our critics. So, we can allow God's words to matter more than accusations from our critics. We obtain our worth from our heavenly parent, who loves us.

Prayer: *Dear God, help us to root our identity in you rather than what others say. Amen*

Thought for the day: I am God's beloved – that is what defines me.

Michelle Laura Heed (New York, USA)

Getting to know God

Read Matthew 7:7–12

'Ask and it will be given to you; seek and you will find; knock and the door will be opened to you.'
Matthew 7:7 (NIV)

Over 30 years ago, I experienced early-onset menopause. I was a mother and working full-time at a bank while my husband had just changed his career path. Fearing an increased risk of breast cancer, I did not take hormone therapy treatment. As a result, I suffered from many disturbing symptoms.

When I turned to my sister for advice, she suggested that I pray for God's help. I hesitated. Why would God listen to my prayer? I was not even a churchgoer. But she encouraged me to pray with all my heart, not worrying about what God would do. By God's mercy, I gained strength in dealing with my situation after praying faithfully every day. As I found peace amid my challenging symptoms, I began to understand how much God loves me. I started attending Sunday services and studying the Bible with fellowship friends, and I joined our church choir.

All these years God has answered many of my prayers. Looking back, those answers are truly miracles in my life, and my sister was a loving angel sent to me by God. How wonderful it is getting to know God, starting with only a faithful prayer.

Prayer: *Heavenly Father, thank you for people who guide us closer to you. Thank you for always opening the door when we knock. Amen*

Thought for the day: When I face challenges, I will turn to God in prayer.

Shelley C. Wu (California, USA)

A new name

Read Isaiah 62:1–5

The nations shall see your vindication, and all the kings your glory; and you shall be called by a new name that the mouth of the Lord will give.

Isaiah 62:2 (NRSV)

I got into a lot of trouble in school, and my report cards always included comments about my bad behaviour. Because of my actions, those comments described me in ways that were not positive, though they were frequently deserved.

Surprisingly, one teacher thought I was redeemable. She named other traits in her comments and in person that revealed my positive attributes. Naturally, my self-esteem increased. In time, others began to see these positive traits in me as well. This one teacher gave me the confidence to live a new way and cast the old identity aside. This wasn't merely a change of perspective but a transformation from God.

The prophet Isaiah documented a similar situation with Israel. They had sinned, but God was gracious, welcoming them back and providing hope. God gave them a new name. 'Forsaken' was changed to 'My Delight Is in Her' (see Isaiah 62:4).

Israel's righteousness was only possible because God saves and redeems. We are described by God's grace rather than the labels of our own sinful condition. Just as my teacher gave me a new identity, God also restores us so we can reveal God's amazing attributes!

Prayer: *Dear God, thank you for naming us and calling us your own. Help us to live in a way that brings you glory. Amen*

Thought for the day: My identity as God's child is stronger than any label others can give me.

Mike Medeiros (California, USA)

Spiritual nutrition

Read Deuteronomy 6:1–9

Start children off on the way they should go, and even when they are old they will not turn from it.
Proverbs 22:6 (NIV)

When I was about seven years old, my mother became bedridden with tuberculosis, making it impossible for her to take care of my two brothers and me. But still she invested in our spiritual growth. Although she had to rely on others to provide us with physical nutrition, she made sure we received spiritual nutrition. She would write down the Lord's Prayer, the ten commandments and Psalm 23 for us to learn. She would give us Bible verses to memorise every day, and I still remember her face beaming with joy when we spoke those verses aloud for her. She passed on her habit of reading *The Upper Room* devotional every day, and it was through her that we grew in faith.

My mother's commitment to our spiritual growth became one of her most important legacies. After she died, we held on to our faith and grew into an even stronger relationship with God. This closeness to God has helped us through times of grief and other challenges of life.

Even though our mother was with us for only a short period of time, I am grateful that she taught us how to praise and serve God. Just as my mother encouraged us in our faith, we can be mentors to others as they grow in faith.

Prayer: *Loving Father, thank you for the gift of those who love and care for us physically and spiritually. In Jesus' name. Amen*

Thought for the day: How will I offer spiritual nourishment to someone today?

Neeta Nayna Macwan (Gujarat, India)

PRAYER FOCUS: SOMEONE WHO HAS NURTURED MY FAITH

The look

Read Luke 22:54–62

Peter replied, 'Man, I don't know what you're talking about!' Just as he was speaking, the cock crowed. The Lord turned and looked straight at Peter.
Luke 22:60–61 (NIV)

I was bullied in middle school. I was nerdy, I didn't wear cool clothes and I was hopeless at sports. I took solace in my friendship with Tarik, an exchange student from India. Like me, he just didn't seem to fit in. But we had a connection through our common pain.

One day as I walked to school, three football players actually talked to me. I was ecstatic! As we approached the school, I saw Tarik by the doorway. Instantly the football players began to tease him. My desire to be popular was overwhelming, and I'm ashamed to admit I joined them in teasing my friend. I will never forget the look Tarik gave me at that moment. He didn't say a word, but I could see the sense of betrayal and sadness in his eyes.

Peter must have felt deep shame when Jesus looked at him after Peter denied knowing Jesus. But Jesus didn't condemn Peter. Rather, I believe Jesus looked deep into Peter's soul and saw the bold man of God Peter would become. When we feel shame for our mistakes, forgiveness is a prayer away. Jesus always looks upon us with unconditional love.

Prayer: *Loving Saviour, help us to remember that your boundless love and sacrifice cover all our sins. May we look at others the way you do. Amen*

Thought for the day: God is looking at me today with eyes of forgiving love.

Tom Smith (Utah, USA)

More than words

Read John 20:24–29

Be like-minded, be sympathetic, love one another, be compassionate and humble.
1 Peter 3:8 (NIV)

As our instructor talked on and on, I saw a classmate squirm in his seat. During a break, he explained, 'Sitting and listening is so difficult for me. I prefer doing, touching, seeing, smelling and even tasting. I'm an experiential learner.'

While reading today's scripture passage, I recalled that conversation and thought that Thomas must have been an experiential learner. Although traditionally he has been called 'Doubting Thomas,' I think maybe Thomas processed information best by receiving it through a combination of senses. Perhaps the report from the other disciples didn't involve enough of his senses for him to process that information easily. Only by hearing, seeing and touching could Thomas accept Jesus' resurrection.

That same hesitance to accept the gospel sometimes hinders us today. We may regard sermons as boring because words alone exclude the other senses. For some, Communion fills that void through touch and taste. Others enjoy children's sermons that often involve multiple senses.

When we are understanding of those who receive the gospel in different ways, we fulfil the charge in today's quoted scripture. We may need their understanding of our differences too.

Prayer: *Precious Lord, help us to be understanding of the unique ways each person receives your good news. In the name of Jesus. Amen*

Thought for the day: Using all my senses can open me to God's presence.

Mary Hunt Webb (New Mexico, USA)

Prompting

Read Haggai 1:2–5, 12–13

Then Haggai, the Lord's messenger, gave this message of the Lord to the people: 'I am with you,' declares the Lord.
Haggai 1:13 (NIV)

I had no reason to dislike this person – I called him 'that Christian' in my head – but we also didn't have anything in common. I was 20 years older. He was a student. I was a maintenance worker. I'd seen thousands of university students come and go. Very few ever spoke to me. But he did, several times. He even remembered my name. He told me about Jesus and encouraged me to return to church.

'I need to get my life right before I go back to church,' I told him. 'I'll do it later.' I don't know if he believed me. I didn't believe myself.

He must have graduated, because I eventually stopped seeing him around campus. That was 30 years ago, but I never forgot his encouragement. In time, I did return to church, and I'm glad I did. But I continued to wonder, 'What blessings did I miss because my faith was a low priority?'

I remind myself that religion is not a transaction. Even when we ignore God's presence, God loves us regardless. But a relationship with God does require our response. When the Israelites answered, God affirmed, 'I am with you.' Now, through Christ, God is always with us.

Prayer: *Dear Lord, thank you for your unconditional love. Empower us to respond by growing in relationship with you. Amen*

Thought for the day: Today I will look for God's promptings in my conversations with others.

Andrew Michael Ardoin (Louisiana, USA)

Stargazing

Read Genesis 1:14–28

'Those who are wise will shine like the brightness of the heavens, and those who lead many to righteousness, like the stars forever and ever.'
Daniel 12:3 (NIV)

I live in a rural area, and it's relaxing to step outside and gaze at the stars twinkling at night. When a meteor shower is predicted in my area, I stand on my back deck with my head tilted back to look for these 'falling stars'. While standing on the deck with the house behind me, I can see only half of the night sky. There may be meteors in parts of the sky that I'm not able to see.

Thankfully, God sees the whole picture. God created us and knows of our past failures and triumphs. God knows what the future holds for us. '"I know the plans I have for you," declares the Lord, "plans to prosper you and not to harm you, plans to give you hope and a future"' (Jeremiah 29:11). God's hand is upon us every day – loving, guiding, protecting and forgiving us.

God created the heavens and earth, and all plants and animals, including us. We can give thanks that God can see everything as a whole and that each one of us is important to our creator.

Prayer: *Creator God, thank you for having your loving hand upon us each day. Help us focus on you so that we will make choices that bring you honour and glory. Amen*

Thought for the day: Knowing that God sees the whole picture brings me comfort.

Lori Hulvey (Illinois, USA)

Obedience

Read Psalm 111

The fear of the Lord is the beginning of wisdom: a good understanding have all they that do his commandments: his praise endureth forever.
Psalm 111:10 (KJV)

One of my daughters plays on a football team. At her first-ever practice, the coach told her to kick the ball with the side of her foot rather than her toe. My daughter insisted that it was better to use her toe because she could kick the ball harder and faster, and she had always done it that way. They went back and forth for a while until the coach finally told my daughter to try it just once. Reluctantly, she gave it a try and found that she had more control and could still kick the ball far. She was convinced once she tried it.

God's commandments can be like that. We think that we have been doing fine on our own, and often God tells us to do something that is not easy or that does not make sense. We may squirm and try our best to rationalise why that does not apply to us because our circumstances are different. We may forget that God's desire is always for our good. God tells us that understanding comes from obedience. When we follow God's commands, even reluctantly, we experience the blessings that come with obedience.

Prayer: *Dear God, may we always be quick to obey you. Help us remember that your ways are always for our good. Amen*

Thought for the day: Even if it is not what I am used to, I will follow God's ways.

Bob LaForge (New Jersey, USA)

Generosity

Read Luke 6:37–42

'Your eye is the lamp of your body. If your eye is healthy, your whole body is full of light; but if it is not healthy, your body is full of darkness. Therefore consider whether the light in you is not darkness.'
Luke 11:34–35 (NRSV)

It was Christmas morning. I got up, went to the bathroom and found a ring of shaving foam in the sink. 'I hate it when he doesn't rinse the basin,' I thought. Once I was washed and dressed, I went to the top of the stairs and noticed the curtains hooked up on the windowsill. 'I hate it when he doesn't straighten the curtains after drawing them back,' I thought. Downstairs and in the kitchen, I began to prepare breakfast and found the dishcloth had been left balled up in the sink rather than spread out to dry. 'I hate it when…' I stopped mid-thought.

This was the day I was supposed to be celebrating the greatest gift of love the world will ever know, and I could barely contain my irritation at the trivial differences in the way my husband and I do things. I was not looking at my husband with a generous heart.

I determined to change my attitude. Day by day I am seeking Christ's grace and love so that I can attend to my own faults and be more patient with others.

Prayer: *Dear Lord Jesus, help us to learn from you how to be tolerant, forgiving and loving to all whom we meet. Amen*

Thought for the day: When I am frustrated with others, I will focus on God's love for them.

Helen Pain (England, United Kingdom)

Tempest

Read Psalm 91:9–16

Do not fear, for I am with you; do not be dismayed, for I am your God.
Isaiah 41:10 (NIV)

My wife and I stood on the balcony facing the Atlantic Ocean as the roaring wind rattled the palm fronds and large foamy waves crashed on the sand. We had to brace ourselves to keep our balance. We quickly went indoors, our eyes burning from the wind and our skin chilled from the driving rain. The next morning, bright azure skies greeted a glorious sunrise. Small waves lapped at the beach, palm trees fluttered and all was peaceful.

Life can be much the same way. The tempests of serious illness, anxiety, job changes, marital difficulties, relationship challenges, business setbacks and other storms of life threaten our sense of well-being. Our faith may even falter. But throughout the turmoil, God is always with us as promised in Isaiah. Jesus through the Holy Spirit says, 'Be still!' And our hearts and minds can find rest and peace once more.

Prayer: *Lord Jesus, be with us this day, in tempests and in calm. Comfort us with the knowledge that you are always near. Amen*

Thought for the day: God is with me through tempests and struggle, offering peace.

John R. Robinson (Georgia, USA)

To love and to laugh

Read John 4:4–26

Jesus answered her, 'If you knew the gift of God and who it is that asks you for a drink, you would have asked him and he would have given you living water.'
John 4:10 (NIV)

When I was in my early 20s, a neighbour invited me to a church service. The pastor talked about the birth of Jesus, his death and resurrection, and how God wants a relationship with us. As part of the service, the ushers distributed slips of paper for the congregation to write down their prayer requests. I clearly remember mine: to love and to laugh.

Loneliness and guilt had filled me with a crushing sense of unworthiness. Like the Samaritan woman in today's reading, I had made choices that isolated me from my family and friends. And like her, I couldn't imagine why Jesus would want to have anything to do with me.

Yet much to the surprise of the Samaritan woman, Jesus talked to her. Though they were strangers, he displayed intimate knowledge of her life and didn't reject her. He offered her a most amazing gift – living water. Bursting with joy, she left her water jar at the well and hurried into town to share her good news. Her testimony was compelling because her spirit had been completely transformed.

In time, God transformed my life as well and gave me faith in Jesus Christ. And then, because God hears and answers prayer, God filled my life with love and laughter.

Prayer: *Heavenly Father, thank you for the good gifts you give us. Thank you especially for the gift of salvation through your Son, Jesus Christ. Amen*

Thought for the day: God can transform my life.

Elizabeth Erlandson (Nebraska, USA)

God's grace is sufficient

Read 2 Corinthians 12:1–10

[The Lord] said to me, 'My grace is sufficient for you, for my power is made perfect in weakness.' Therefore I will boast all the more gladly about my weaknesses, so that Christ's power may rest on me.
2 Corinthians 12:9 (NIV)

I was in the waiting area being prepared for another surgery. Three other patients were brought in with me. As the nurse was preparing a patient named Raúl, he began to express to the nurse his anxiety about the procedure and the discomfort he had experienced the night before.

Overhearing this short exchange, the words of the apostle Paul above came to my mind. While the nurse prepared my intravenous drip, I was able to chat with Raúl, sharing what I had learned through previous surgeries. I also shared some suggestions he might consider during his recuperation, adding that in spite of our suffering God offers hope. After talking for a couple more minutes, we prayed together. As Raúl was wheeled into surgery, he appeared much more serene.

I was also comforted, knowing that God was by my side and that what I had learned as a result of my previous surgeries opened the door to offer some help, perhaps even a blessing, to someone else. When we place our full trust in Christ, we are called by the Spirit to be open to help others wherever we are. We can live out our faith, confident in the knowledge that our creator knows our every need and that God's grace is sufficient.

Prayer: *God of mercy, even in our weakness we remain confident that your grace is sufficient for us and we, in turn, can be attentive to the needs of others. In Jesus' name. Amen*

Thought for the day: God's grace is with us today and always.

Nelly García Gallardo (Mexico City, Mexico)

Giving from the heart

Read Matthew 18:1–5

Whosoever therefore shall humble himself as this little child, the same is greatest in the kingdom of heaven.
Matthew 18:4 (KJV)

While attending a book fair at my oldest grandson's primary school, I witnessed an act of kindness that warmed my heart. Andrew, my grandson, had earned money to spend at the book fair by helping his mother at home. He chose a couple of books and made his purchase. He had money left over, but one of his friends didn't have any money.

His young companion had picked up a couple of books and was about to put them back. Andrew made eye contact with me and I could tell he was seeking my approval. He wanted to purchase the books for his friend. I told Andrew he had earned the money so it was his to spend, but yes, it would be nice to share. And he did.

When I witness acts of kindness, especially from children, it renews my faith in the Lord and assures me that God is at work in the world. Praise be to God for acts of kindness that reveal God's presence.

Prayer: *Dear Lord, thank you for the children in our lives who teach us about your unselfish, genuine love. Help us to become more like them. Amen*

Thought for the day: How do those around me teach me about Jesus?

Larry Dowell (North Carolina, USA)

A place for us

Read John 14:1–7

See what great love the Father has lavished on us, that we should be called children of God!
1 John 3:1 (NIV)

For most of my life, I have struggled with anxiety. I pile up stresses for myself, and I think of life like I'm running a race with a goal of winning something – good grades, athletic achievement or being the best at my favourite activities.

In high school, one such goal was to fit in. This goal turned out to be unachievable for several reasons. My limited finances, transportation and dislike of texting conversations made me unfit to join the group I wanted to be a part of.

At the time I didn't recognise that, even though I struggled to fit in in high school, I was already included in an even more important group: God's family. This family did not have earthly requirements like the group in high school. This family only needed my love, faith and belief in the greatest good of all. It does not matter to God where we are from, how much money we have or if our life is perfect in the world's eyes. God cares and has a place for every one of us – Jesus himself has prepared it! This promise gives me comfort and a new appreciation for my wonderfully unique and diverse family.

Prayer: *Dear God, help us to realise that we are your family and that is what matters most. Amen*

Thought for the day: I always fit in, because I am part of God's loving family.

Josey McChesney (Missouri, USA)

A deep search

Read Psalm 139:1–12

Search me, God, and know my heart; test me and know my anxious thoughts. See if there is any offensive way in me, and lead me in the way everlasting.
Psalm 139:23–24 (NIV)

One day my husband asked me if I had seen his notepad. I suggested that he check under the cushion of his favourite chair, where things often slide out of sight. He assured me that he had already looked there, but I decided to check again in case the notebook had slipped too deep for his larger hands to reach. I pulled off the seat cushion and found a few crumbs. I put my hand deeper into the chair and pulled out an empty bag, a few old wrappers, some wadded up tissue, several old magazines and finally a fork – but no notebook.

My search in the chair reminded me of the importance of searching my heart and life. The chair looked clean at first glance. It took a deep search to find the hidden items lurking in the depths. Similarly, others may take a superficial glance at me and not see the crumbs of sinful acts and emotions that hide below the surface.

The psalmist begged God to search him and know his heart and anxious thoughts. I need to allow God's light to shine into the corners of my heart too. God will help me to clean up whatever is there.

Prayer: *Dear God, thank you for your steadfast love. Search our hearts and lives, and help us always to be obedient to you. Amen*

Thought for the day: God's light can illumine even the darkest corners of my life.

Carol Harrison (Saskatchewan, Canada)

Past, present and future

Read Acts 12:6–17

'Therefore I tell you, whatever you ask for in prayer, believe that you have received it, and it will be yours.'
Mark 11:24 (NIV)

When my wife was hospitalised after a stroke, a church group gave her a blanket embroidered with her name and Mark 11:24. When I looked up the verse, it gave me hope. Along with our friends and our church, I was fervently praying for my wife's complete recovery. When she died seven weeks later, I was grief-stricken. Not only did I lose my wife, but our prayers had not been granted. I felt like I had failed. Surely if I had been more faithful, God would have healed my wife.

For years I have wrestled with this verse. The mix of past and future tenses is puzzling. I believe prayer changes things, but this passage teaches me that our prayers are never *just* about the future. Praying conforms us to God's will in the present. We are comforted in this transformation by looking to God's faithfulness in the past. Further, like the disciples in Acts 12, sometimes we don't immediately recognise the answer to our prayers.

I'm still mourning the loss of my wife, but slowly I am beginning to appreciate the profound ways God answers my prayers – ways so amazing that I don't always understand them. I have come to accept that God doesn't require my understanding, just my steadfast, faithful confidence in God's love for me.

Prayer: *Dear Lord, help us to see the ways you have guided us in the past, and grant us faith to trust our futures to you, no matter what is happening in the present. Amen*

Thought for the day: How has God acted in my past?

Bill Kirklin (Indiana, USA)

Learning to trust

Read Psalm 94:16–19

When anxiety was great within me, your consolation brought me joy.
Psalm 94:19 (NIV)

Many times I have stressed over things beyond my control. I began to ask myself, 'Why? Do I doubt God?' Then my friend suggested that when I felt stressed and worried over something, I should write it down, put it in a 'God Box,' and stop fretting about it.

One day when I was stressing over things I could not control, I tried it. I wrote my worry on a piece of scrap paper, prayed, cried and put it in the box. I may have prayed a few more times, but eventually I forgot it. Whenever a new issue came up, I put it in the box. And when I eventually decided to empty the God Box, I couldn't remember a single thing I had written!

Over the years, I have grown in my faith and no longer need a physical God Box. I am better able to surrender my worries to God and trust that God cares for my concerns. I realise now that the answer to my earlier question is that I wasn't trusting God. But God has always cared for me. I have learned to trust more and doubt less with renewed hope and joy.

Prayer: *Dear God, in our times of need, open our eyes to your love and faithfulness. Help us to grow in our faith by surrendering our struggles to you. In Jesus' name. Amen*

Thought for the day: I can grow in my faith by trusting God with my concerns.

Doreen Alvarez (Florida, USA)

The power of words

Read James 3:9–18

Let the words of my mouth and the meditation of my heart be acceptable to you, O Lord, my rock and my redeemer.
Psalm 19:14 (NRSV)

Words are powerful. Some words are a balm to our soul while other words cut like a sharp knife. In an environment where God's Spirit does not abound, hurtful or destructive words often prevail.

Followers of Christ are called to reflect our faith in word and deed. Our teacher, Jesus, spoke words of comfort where there was loss, forgiveness where there was fault, solution where there was conflict, life where there was death, peace and hope where there was fear and anxiety. On several occasions Jesus spoke with compassion that changed lives forever.

Today, someone we know may need to hear words of hope, faith and life. We can follow Jesus' example and use the power of words to share the good news.

Prayer: *Fine-tune our words, O God, so that others will know that we are followers of Christ. We pray as Jesus taught us, 'Our Father in heaven, hallowed be your name, your kingdom come, your will be done on earth as it is in heaven. Give us today our daily bread. Forgive us our debts, as we also have forgiven our debtors. And lead us not into temptation, but deliver us from the evil one.'* Amen*

Thought for the day: Today I will speak words of hope by sharing the good news of Jesus Christ.

Julianis Báez de Pichardo (Dominican Republic)

PRAYER FOCUS: SOMEONE HURT BY MY WORDS
*Matthew 6:9–13 (NIV)

God's timing

Read Ecclesiastes 3:9–13

Many are the plans in a person's heart, but it is the Lord's purpose that prevails.
Proverbs 19:21 (NIV)

Earlier in my career as a speech-language pathologist, I received yearly contracts to work in a particular school district. One year, when July rolled around, I had no contract. Reluctantly, I took work at a nursing facility. I was deeply unsatisfied, but my wife told me repeatedly, 'It's only a season.'

In March of that year, we discovered a lump in my wife's breast. Over the next ten months, we went to dozens of doctors' appointments and treatments. We prayed constantly. Eventually, my wife's initial treatment was complete. She was cancer-free!

I missed only two medical appointments during those months. Working at the nursing facility made that possible because my schedule was flexible. Had I worked at a school, I wouldn't have been able to be with my wife when she needed me most. I believe that by putting me in the nursing facility, the Lord was nurturing us long before we even realised we needed it. Sometimes when I don't understand what God is doing, I think about that experience. I remember that God can use the pieces of my life to help me end up exactly where I need to be.

Prayer: *O Lord, help us to remember that you are forever faithful, even when we can't see the bigger picture. In Jesus' name. Amen*

Thought for the day: Even when I don't fully understand, I will trust God.

R.G. Wood (Ohio, USA)

I can hear you, Lord

Read Psalm 25:1–7

We are God's handiwork, created in Christ Jesus to do good works, which God prepared in advance for us to do.
Ephesians 2:10 (NIV)

I remember sitting in church as a child and wondering if I would ever hear God's voice. I couldn't recall a time when I knew God was talking to me. As the years passed, I stopped listening, and I didn't talk to God much.

Then in my 20s as a mum of two, I started praying more often. I talked to God every night at bedtime and throughout each day, asking for patience and guidance. Soon I started hearing God's replies. I noticed that the more I talked to God, the more I sensed God talking to me – sometimes in answers to prayer, sometimes through small signs of God's presence and sometimes by showing me things God wanted me to do.

I heard God urging me to take a cake to a church lunch or to drop off a plate of goodies for a grieving loved one. I recognised that God was urging me to use my gifts to do God's work. After spending so many years thinking that I would never hear God's voice, hearing God in these ways encouraged me and strengthened my relationship with God. I began to talk to God more – thanking God for small blessings and asking for strength, patience or forgiveness when I fell short of the mum, wife and Christian that I desire to be.

Prayer: *Dear God, help us to hear you, to do your work and to talk to you more each day. Amen*

Thought for the day: Today I will talk to God as I go about my daily tasks.

Megan Vollmer (Wisconsin, USA)

A heart filled with joy

Read Hebrews 12:1–3

Let us also lay aside every weight and the sin that clings so closely, and let us run with perseverance the race that is set before us, looking to Jesus the pioneer and perfecter of our faith, who for the sake of the joy that was set before him endured the cross.
Hebrews 12:1–2 (NRSV)

I have recently enjoyed watching a show where a consultant helps people declutter and tidy up their homes. The consultant's method is to only have items in the home that spark joy. Clients go through every item they own. If the item sparks joy, they keep it, and if it doesn't, they get rid of it. It is satisfying to see the joy people feel afterward, when they no longer have clutter in their homes.

This got me thinking about the clutter we all have – not in our homes, but in our hearts. Perhaps it's a comment someone made years ago that we keep replaying in our minds, or the disappointment we felt when we weren't given an opportunity, or resentment towards someone for a wrong they did. But I believe God wants to declutter our hearts. What if we refuse to dwell on or be hindered by the memories, behaviours or thoughts that don't spark joy in our lives?

As Hebrews 12:1–3 tells us, we can do this by looking to Jesus as our example. Jesus was betrayed and tortured. Yet the Bible tells us that because of the joy before him, he endured. Joy gives us the endurance we need to run our race and to get through the tough times.

Prayer: *Dear Lord, show us the things in our hearts that don't spark joy, and help us release them to you. Help us to run our race with joy and endurance. Amen*

Thought for the day: Today I will let go of the clutter in my heart so that I can better serve God.

Shelley Marolla (Victoria, Australia)

Through the fog

Read 1 Samuel 3:2–11

The Lord came and stood there, calling as at the other times, 'Samuel! Samuel!' Then Samuel said, 'Speak, for your servant is listening.'
1 Samuel 3:10 (NIV)

Travelling through a thick fog, I was listening to a devotional programme based on the calling of Samuel. The speaker gave an invitation simply to pray Samuel's prayer, 'Speak, Lord, for your servant is listening.' Then we were to be silent and listen.

The road on which I was travelling was crooked, and the thick fog created even more danger. I passed fields and thickets of trees from which deer could easily veer into my path. I cautiously navigated the road ahead and prayed, 'Speak, Lord, for your servant is listening.'

God spoke by revealing how that moment was a great analogy for how to live by faith. I thought about how often it feels as if we are living in a fog, enveloped in the cares of our world while doing our best to follow the path before us. Then God reminded me that, though the road ahead can be dark and winding, the light of Christ is always with us, leading us to where we need to be.

I realised in that moment that if I trust the guiding light of God's care, I will ultimately be okay. I did make it safely to my destination, with the words of Samuel still echoing in my mind: 'Speak, Lord, for your servant is listening.'

Prayer: *O God, be forever the light before us and the voice that calls us. Help us to listen and respond. In Jesus' name. Amen*

Thought for the day: How do I take time to listen for God's voice?

Tim Tate (Virginia, USA)

Singing praises

Read Psalm 100

Sing to the Lord with thanks; sing praises to our God with a lyre!
Psalm 147:7 (CEB)

As the new board chair of a campus ministry, I was excited to work along-side the eager student-led worship team. We met one Saturday a month to plan weekly services. I was amazed and encouraged by the dedication of the students who were willing to share their faith with their peers.

Each meeting opened with songs of worship. As I'm not musically inclined, I thought these sessions were entirely too long. I felt that the songs took up too much time that could be better spent in planning and training.

After a few months of these gatherings, my attitude began to shift. I found that the music moved me in a way that sermons and Bible studies often did not. The music I had once considered a traditional formality became a form of deep and meaningful worship for me. The Lord opened my heart during my years of service with this group, and I felt God's love on a deeper level than I'd ever experienced.

Now whenever the choir or worship band begins their praise music, I recall the scriptures that teach us to sing out our thanks and praises to God. Even with my limited musical talents, I happily make a joyful noise to the Lord.

Prayer: *Holy Father, help us to hear your voice during our times of worship. Amen*

Thought for the day: Today I will worship God with joy and thanksgiving.

Bobbie Smith Bryant (Kentucky, USA)

Who is my neighbour?

Read Luke 10:25–37

Wanting to justify himself, [the lawyer] asked Jesus, 'And who is my neighbour?'

Luke 10:29 (NRSV)

In response to the lawyer's question in today's scripture reading, Jesus offers a parable which encourages us to show solidarity and compassion for fellow human beings, regardless of the circumstances. This mandate is similar to the mission that firefighters in Chile have always followed. In Chile, all who serve as firefighters are volunteers and take to heart the mission to 'love your neighbour'. Those who volunteer as firefighters are willing to give their lives for others if necessary.

Having served as a firefighter for more than 65 years, I have witnessed many tragedies where families have lost homes, belongings and family members to fires. Tragedy is everywhere, though. People all over the world have experienced earthquakes, tsunamis, devastating storms and the Covid-19 pandemic that has ravaged the world. Firefighters and other dedicated personnel, especially in the field of health services, continue to struggle to help our neighbours. All of us can remain committed to loving our neighbours because the call to love God and neighbour is Jesus' greatest commandment.

Prayer: *Your words are written on our hearts, O God. Embolden our resolve to show our love for you by helping our neighbours. Amen*

Thought for the day: Today I will follow Jesus' commandment to love my neighbour.

Luis Pastén Pastén (Antofagasta, Chile)

Slow swim

Read Matthew 9:35–38

Jesus went through all the towns and villages, teaching in their synagogues.
Matthew 9:35 (NIV)

Recently a friend and I joined a wild swimming club, fulfilling a dream. The first day, we waded into the crystal clear lake, splashed in and swam. Slowly.

It's impossible to say how many people overtook us. Gliding past effortlessly in full wetsuit and goggles, they seemed not just a different kind of swimmer, but a completely different species. As they sped past, the feeling was all too familiar. I have always felt like I'm trailing behind, being overtaken by the speedy ones and struggling to keep afloat in their after-current. Work, relationships, house-buying, parenthood – I always seem to get there last. It's a humbling experience and I deal with it better in swimming than I do in life.

In the lake, however, we enjoyed our slow pace, chatting as we swam, admiring wagtails and gasping at newly hatched ducklings. It dawned on me that this is also how I live my life when I don't rush, when I stop worrying about who is going faster than me.

I think of Jesus, wandering from town to village. I imagine there was nothing speedy or go-getting about it. He took time to see people, to listen, to help. Then I realise my slow journey through life is not such a disaster. I may not achieve as much or as quickly as some, but perhaps, in my slowness, I can relish God's beauty and presence, taking time for whatever he has in store for me.

Prayer: *Jesus, help us to slow down and appreciate the work and the beauty you have planned for us. Amen*

Thought for the day: What am I rushing past?

Clare O'Driscoll (England, United Kingdom)

Immeasurable God

Read Psalm 147:1–11

Great is our Lord, and abundant in power; his understanding is beyond measure.
Psalm 147:5 (NRSV)

While talking with my wife at dinner, I asked her about the value of pi (π) – the number that starts out 3.14159. It is used for calculating the circumference and area of a circle. My wife, a maths teacher, affirmed that pi is an 'irrational number,' meaning that it goes on and on. While no mathematician can fully write out the endless series of digits that comprise pi, it is nonetheless vitally important for calculations made by engineers, inventors, artists and even chefs.

Like pi, God is also immeasurable in that we cannot fathom the fullness of who God is. Yet knowing God helps us to make sense of life. We may spend a lifetime calculating the infinite 'digits' of God, each one of which brings new wonder, surprise and perspective to our search to know God. But knowing that God is immeasurable can bring us comfort because the God who holds infinite knowledge in one hand also holds endless love in the other.

Today we can rejoice, knowing that while God spans far beyond human understanding, God gives us enough 'digits' to know abundant beauty and profound love.

Prayer: *Immeasurable God, thank you for allowing us to catch a glimpse of who you are. Help us to trust you far beyond our own understanding. Amen*

Thought for the day: Though I cannot fully comprehend God, I trust God's power and love.

Luke Ecklund Heberle (Ohio, USA)

Embracing uncertainty

Read Matthew 6:25–34

Faith is confidence in what we hope for and assurance about what we do not see.
Hebrews 11:1 (NIV)

One day I began to feel disturbed by thoughts of what my future might look like. I wondered if I had made a wrong choice, and I felt confused and overwhelmed with fear. I asked God to speak to me and help me, but I felt the same. I tried to recall a scripture verse that would help me, but I could not remember one. I began to lose hope.

Later I saw a post on social media that contained the word 'uncertainty' and a reference to Hebrews 11:1. I quickly turned to the verse and read it again and again. I learned that by embracing my uncertainty with faith, my fears lessened.

I often want to know what my future will look like, and I worry about choices I have made regarding my career or education. But scripture reminds me that faith will enable me to let go of my fear and trust God.

Hebrews 11 reminds us that whenever we feel disturbed and stressed about the future or our choices, we can put our faith in God, who holds our future and wants the best for us. With this assurance we can embrace uncertainty with faith and encourage others to do the same.

Prayer: *Dear Lord, please help us to have faith in you and to let go of fear as we entrust the future to you. Amen*

Thought for the day: I trust that God has a good plan for my future.

Keren Philips (Karnataka, India)

Redemption

Read Isaiah 55:6–9

There is a time for everything, and a season for every activity under the heavens.
Ecclesiastes 3:1 (NIV)

I was in high school when my mother died after a long battle with cancer. I was not only sad; I was also angry with God. I couldn't see any purpose in what had happened, and I questioned God's wisdom and even God's existence. Though my grief subsided, the question 'Why?' still remained deep inside me. Whenever others mentioned their mothers, my hurt resurfaced.

After graduation from college, I became a high school chemistry teacher – a job I loved. I had been teaching for about 20 years when a student returned to class after missing a week of school because of the death of a parent. What was to be an hour of helping her catch up became an opportunity to empathise with her. I told her I had been about her age when my mother died, and I shared with her the hurt I had felt when other kids mentioned their mothers. She looked at me with tears in her eyes and said, 'Thank you, Mr B. No one else seems to understand.' Because of my own experience, I was able to offer her comfort and support. At that moment I finally found something redeeming in the grief I had felt at my mother's death and for the decades since. And I understood that when we grieve, God grieves with us.

Prayer: *Father God, thank you for being with us as we grieve. Teach us patience as we learn to trust you in all things. Amen*

Thought for the day: My experiences equip me to show God's comfort to others.

Brad Butler (North Carolina, USA)

Looking closely

Read Proverbs 2:1–8

Happy are those who find wisdom and those who gain understanding.
Proverbs 3:13 (CEB)

Having low vision sometimes hinders me, but it also forces me to look more closely at things. Since I can't always trust my depth perception, I occasionally rely on touch to navigate. One evening at a church prayer meeting, I was making my way along the wall behind the altar. The wall has a large cross painted on it, and the cross was right beside me. Out of the corner of my eye, I noticed a tiny line of delicate gold script hidden along the dark brown vertical edge of the cross. Upon further investigation, I found that it was inscribed, 'Jesus Christ is forever Lord of lords and King of kings.' I pointed out my discovery to the others at the prayer meeting, and each of them admitted that they had never noticed the inscription. We concluded that the phrase was put there by an artist who understood that – like many of God's marvelous truths – it would only be discovered by a close examination.

Following that experience, I decided that I needed to become much more diligent in my study of God's word and in my prayer life. Wisdom and understanding are available to all, but those who look closely will find deeper beauty.

Prayer: *Heavenly Father, thank you for giving us scripture. As we read it, help us to slow down and look for the beauty and truth in every verse. Amen*

Thought for the day: Today I will take time to look for God's beauty and truth.

Geo Pickell (North Dakota, USA)

Sharing blessings

Read 1 Corinthians 9:19–23

I do all this for the sake of the gospel, that I may share in its blessings.
1 Corinthians 9:23 (NIV)

I began visiting a young woman who lived in a poor, run-down part of town. She had been ill and in bed for days, and she did not have anyone to take care of her. Every time I visited, she asked me to sing a song and read the Bible to her.

On each visit, she listened quietly and never spoke. Then one day she whispered to me, 'Thank you for treating me like a human being. I can feel the love of Jesus this week. Please ask him to receive me as his daughter. I trust that Jesus is my Saviour, and I want to receive him before I go home. Please ask Jesus to bring me to my eternal home in heaven.'

Not long after praying, she went home to her Father in heaven. The apostle Paul wrote that he wanted to make himself a slave to everyone, even though he was free. He did this for the sake of the gospel and so shared in its blessings. Jesus wants us to use our great potential as a blessing for many people, not for our own sake but for the sake of the gospel.

Prayer: *Dear Jesus, thank you for opportunities to serve you and to show your love to others. Amen*

Thought for the day: By humbling myself to serve others, I can be God's blessing to many.

Linda Chandra (Banten, Indonesia)

God's light in me

Read John 1:1–14

The light shines in the darkness, and the darkness has not overcome it.
John 1:5 (NIV)

For several years I lived in a place where electricity could not be depended on. Most days we had electricity for three or four hours in the evening, but when the electricity abruptly went off there was total darkness. On clear nights the stars of the Milky Way and the moon provided light, but on cloudy nights the darkness was complete. I often woke up in the night, heard the howls of packs of dogs or wolves, and felt suffocated by the darkness.

On one of these cold, dark nights I woke up in paralysing fear. Then some words of scripture came to my mind reminding me that God is light and is the source of all light. I realised that because I belong to God and God's light is in me, I always carry that light even when I may not be able to physically see it. I went back to sleep that night, feeling comforted.

I have carried this lesson with me, and God is my constant light within. I am tempted to fear when I see the evil in the world, but scripture again reminds me that God's light dwells in me. I can find peace in God's light and shine it so that others can find peace when darkness seems to be closing in.

Prayer: *Thank you, Father, for the gift of light you have given us through your Son. Amen*

Thought for the day: God's light is always in me, because I belong to God.

Jerry White (Florida, USA)

Send me!

Read Isaiah 6:1–8

I heard the voice of the Lord saying, 'Whom shall I send? And who will go for us?' And I said, 'Here am I. Send me!'
Isaiah 6:8 (NIV)

My husband and I had served as youth helpers for two years when our pastor approached us about the need for a youth pastor at a small church across the state. My initial response was, 'No way!' I had no formal education or training, and I had left that area after a tumultuous childhood. I had no desire to return to a place where I had felt judged and isolated, yet my heart desired to live for Jesus and I felt him calling. So we answered the call. Of course when we said, 'Send us,' ours was more like a frightened mumble than a shout, but we said yes.

Though it proved challenging, I'll never regret our response. God moved in mighty ways through us. We were able to launch a youth group and brought teens from different denominations together for camps, offering them a sense of belonging. Through outreach efforts, we also saw significant transformation in the lives of many imprisoned youth. I'm still amazed at the powerful ways God used us, with all our imperfections. From this time in my life, I learned that God doesn't need the smartest or most talented people to transform the world. God simply needs someone willing to say, 'Send me.'

Prayer: *Dear God, help each of us to be willing to say yes to you. Give us the strength to serve you in whatever ways we can. Amen*

Thought for the day: When I say yes, God can do great things through me.

Katie J. Trent (Arizona, USA)

New shoots

Read John 11:38–44

Jesus said to [Martha], 'I am the resurrection and the life. Those who believe in me, even though they die, will live, and everyone who lives and believes in me will never die. Do you believe this?'
John 11:25–26 (NRSV)

Beautiful Queen of the Night flowers grew in our yard. My family loved to stay up late and enjoy their pleasant fragrance. However, during last year's dry season, a fire destroyed every plant around our house. We did not expect to be able to enjoy those flowers again, but as the rains started falling this year, new and beautiful shoots of this wonderful plant surprisingly sprouted in the yard.

The shoots had died in the fire, but the roots remained safe in the ground until the rains brought them new life. This made me think about how God, through Christ, renews us. We can trust God and patiently wait like the roots of our Queen of the Night flower. Even when we miss opportunities, experience delays or our prayers are not answered as we expect, we always have the hope of new life when we remain rooted in Christ.

Prayer: *Dear Lord, help us to trust in you even when we don't see your presence. Grant us patience, for we know you can bring new life out of every situation. As Jesus taught us, we pray, 'Our Father which art in heaven, Hallowed be thy name. Thy kingdom come. Thy will be done in earth, as it is in heaven. Give us this day our daily bread. And forgive us our debts, as we forgive our debtors. And lead us not into temptation, but deliver us from evil: For thine is the kingdom, and the power, and the glory, forever.'* Amen*

Thought for the day: I trust that God can always bring new life.

Olaiya Muyiwa Benralph (Federal Capital Territory, Nigeria)

PRAYER FOCUS: THOSE WHO ARE STRUGGLING TO HOPE
*Matthew 6:9–13 (KJV)

Perfect peace

Read Psalm 23

Thou wilt keep him in perfect peace, whose mind is stayed on thee: because he trusteth in thee.
Isaiah 26:3 (KJV)

Roughly two years ago, my doctors discovered I had breast cancer, and I spent the following year fighting the disease. During that time, I suffered. I asked everyone to pray and then kept to myself, turning inward. I wrestled with the unknown and felt sick from the chemotherapy. My husband supported me completely, fielding calls from loved ones and friends when I was feeling too tired or sad. For months I've now been enjoying relatively good health. That changed several weeks ago when I was diagnosed with metastatic breast cancer.

I want it to be different this time, but metastatic cancer is not something that can be cured. Even if I enter remission, the cancer will eventually return. I'm only 66, and I really thought I had this beat. My days and nights alternate between relative calm and complete anguish. How will I tell my loved ones? What will my husband do without me? What do I do about my beloved cats and dog?

Trusting in the Holy Spirit, I know one thing: God has been and will be with me every step of the way. And I know I will be with my creator in eternal life. When my worries become overwhelming, God is there to share my burden.

Prayer: *Merciful God, we surrender our lives to you. May we live for your glory. And when it is time to die, may we die in faith. Amen*

Thought for the day: When troubles overwhelm me, God will ease my burden.

Belinda Voigtmann (Missouri, USA)

PRAYER FOCUS: THOSE LIVING WITH A TERMINAL ILLNESS

Loving God

Read 1 John 4:16–19
We love because [God] first loved us.
1 John 4:19 (NRSV)

One February morning, I walked into the church's daycare centre and found the room filled with valentines – red hearts, pink hearts, hearts adorned with paper doilies, hearts cut from magazines. They hung from the ceiling; they were posted on bulletin boards and taped to windows; they were scattered on tables. I commented to the director about the delightful display. 'Oh,' she explained, 'these are valentines that the children made for God.' What a wonderful idea!

Every February, my wife and I send Valentine's Day cards to our grand-children to let them know that we love them. But too often I fail to express my love to God. My love for God is a response to God's divine love for me. We can express our love for God by spending time in God's presence, enjoying God's nearness, reading God's word, and daily seeking to know God better. We also show our love for God in the way we talk, what we do and how we use our talents.

Every day is made up of hundreds of little moments that are oppor-tunities to love God, and every opportunity matters. I try to include in my morning prayers some verbal 'valentine' and, in my daily activities, demonstrations to God that are a simple 'I love you' to the One who first loved me.

Prayer: *Loving God, we want to know you and be known by you. May your love radiate from us so that others will know your love. Amen*

Thought for the day: I will be intentional about showing my love for God today.

Drexel C. Rankin (Kentucky, USA)

A gentle heart

Read Matthew 11:28–30

Let your gentleness be evident to all. The Lord is near.
Philippians 4:5 (NIV)

I am a driven person. I thrive on achieving new things and checking items off my daily to-do list. I was competitive early in my childhood, even over simple games like musical chairs. As I grew older, I began to believe the message that we must always bring our best to everything we do, and even that we must always *be* the best.

In many ways I have been rewarded for my drive throughout my life. But what few people know is how hard I am on myself. I can be my own worst critic, examining everything I say and do for flaws. I scrutinise my performance at work, at home, in ministry and in my relationships. And I expect more from myself than anyone else ever does.

Lately God has been showing me another way. Jesus had a difficult mission to accomplish, but his approach made all the difference. Jesus had a calm and gentle spirit, and from this wellspring of divine love flowed acts of kindness, healing and restoration. I think God wants us to pursue worthy goals and plans. But first, God wants to show us that how we go about pursuing them is just as important.

Prayer: *Dear God, as we pursue goals in life, teach us to be gentle with ourselves and others. Amen*

Thought for the day: When I am weighed down by self-criticism, I will remember to be gentle like Jesus.

Piyumi Kapugeekiyana (Western Province, Sri Lanka)

Loneliness

Read Matthew 22:34–40

'You shall love your neighbour as yourself.'
Matthew 22:39 (NRSV)

Social media has captivated our world. The Internet and wireless communications have created unprecedented global interaction. But in spite of this connection, our society is experiencing a surge of loneliness.

In response to this loneliness, there are now programmes in large metropolitan areas to encourage socialising. The UK even has a minister for loneliness to combat social isolation and reduce associated health risks. These are new public strategies to battle loneliness, but what is my personal strategy as a Christian?

The obvious one is to love my neighbour as myself. Jesus told us that the greatest commandments are to love God and to love others. But this law of love often illuminates my shortcomings. In stores, doctors' offices, my neighbourhood or other public places, I can easily become self-absorbed and oblivious to those around me – sometimes while on my phone. Instead of connecting with those who physically cross my path, I become captivated by virtual connections. I now pray for help to be present in the moment and attentively greet the people around me. Our individual efforts to live Jesus' commandment and ease loneliness in our world can feel insignificant. But when Christians truly seek to love God and love others, we can make a real difference.

Prayer: *Dear Jesus, help us to live your commandment to love you and to love others. Amen*

Thought for the day: Today I will show God's love by greeting people I meet.

Beverly Taylor (Arizona, USA)

I will forgive

Read John 8:2–11

'Woman, where are they? Has no one condemned you?' 'No one, sir,'
she said. 'Then neither do I condemn you,' Jesus declared. 'Go now
and leave your life of sin.'
John 8:10–11 (NIV)

I recently found my university residence hall completely trashed. Chairs
were strewn all over; broken eggs were splattered on everything; toilet
paper coated most surfaces. I was livid.

I told anyone who would listen how mad I was, and I wanted to get
back at the people who had done this. Thankfully, the time it took to
clean up cleared my head, and I was reminded of the story from John 8.

Though the woman had sinned, Jesus implicated the Pharisees, saying
'any one of you who is without sin be the first to throw a stone' (John 8:7).
Jesus called attention to the fact that we are all sinners and chose to
forgive the woman instead of shaming or punishing her. That is love,
that is forgiveness, and that is the God we follow.

The pranksters did something wrong, but it is not my place to condemn them. If I want to become like Christ, then I need to forgive people,
even when they have wronged me. I must forgive because Jesus first
forgave me.

Prayer: *Dear God, help us be faithful to you in our forgiveness. Help us*
find it in our hearts to forgive those who have wronged us. Amen

Thought for the day: I will follow Christ's teaching and forgive my
enemies today.

Matthew Holden (Indiana, USA)

There is hope

Read Psalm 63:1–8

Because you are my help, I sing in the shadow of your wings.
Psalm 63:7 (NIV)

'One, two, three, four…' As the test administrator counted aloud my incorrect answers, I knew that I had failed the provisional driver licence exam. I had done so much in preparation for the exam. I had thoroughly studied the learner's licence handbook. I had taken pictures to go on my licence, and I had paid for the exam. 'Where did I go wrong?' I kept asking myself.

I dragged my feet on the way to tell my parents. I decided that I was so hurt that I would not retake the test any time soon. It took me a year before I decided to try again. During that time I came across this verse: 'For there is hope of a tree, if it be cut down, that it will sprout again, and that the tender branch thereof will not cease' (Job 14:7, KJV). I realised there was hope. I had not passed before, but I could try again. I retook the exam, and by the grace of God, I passed!

We all face situations or seasons that make us lose hope. Sometimes we try our best, and it is not enough. But God is forever ready to help us keep going. When we want to give up, let us surrender our situation to God with hope that God will see us through.

Prayer: *God of hope, we call upon your name and your help in our times of need. When we want to give up, help us to keep going. In Jesus' name. Amen*

Thought for the day: When I fail, I will look to God for help and try again.

Vimbai Chizarura (Mashonaland East, Zimbabwe)

The gift of one another

Read 1 Thessalonians 2:9–13

Remember your leaders, who spoke the word of God to you. Consider the outcome of their way of life and imitate their faith.
Hebrews 13:7 (NIV)

My son is barely four years old, but everything about him – from the clothes he wears to his brand new 'big-boy haircut' – reminds me of myself. On Sundays after morning worship, he confidently strides on to the stage to join me and bang on my drums. You can see clearly that he wants to be just like his dad.

We sometimes can be hesitant to emulate another person too closely. Maybe we're nervous about idolising another person, or we're terrified at the thought that someone may be looking up to us! However, we may be missing out on one of the greatest gifts God has given us for our spiritual growth – the gift of one another.

In 1 Thessalonians, Paul commends the church for imitating more mature believers, who put their trust in God's word. Mature believers imitate God, and by emulating mature believers we can mature in faith as well.

As we walk the path of faith together, we need not be afraid to find someone we can look to just as my son looks up to me. We need not be afraid to follow the example of the faithful role models God gives us – the ones who imitate Christ. As we walk arm-in-arm with other believers, together we learn to become just like our heavenly Father.

Prayer: *Dear Lord, surround us with people who can help us grow closer to you. Then help us to lead others in the way that leads to mature faith. Amen*

Thought for the day: Who is my role model in following Christ?

Jason Koon (North Carolina, USA)

Following in faith

Read Luke 1:46–55

Mary said, 'With all my heart I glorify the Lord! In the depths of who I am I rejoice in God my saviour.'
Luke 1:46–47 (CEB)

Several months after our wedding, my husband felt called into ministry. Pursuing this vocation required a huge shift in our finances and priorities. Every step we took was one of total faith, and it was one of the scariest things that I have ever done.

When I met my husband, neither of us knew what God's plan was for us. In many ways, we still do not know entirely where God will send us. And as someone who loves to plan, trusting in God's design and accepting that it may not align with mine is scary.

I have found great comfort in Mary's prayer after she learned from the angel Gabriel that she would be the mother of Christ. She glorifies God and accepts without hesitation the future that has been presented to her. What a great example for us today!

Glorifying God in uncertainty and following in obedience into an unknown future becomes easier when I remember Jesus Christ is always with me. Philippians 4:13 reminds me that I can do all things through Christ. Trusting his promises helps me take those steps of faith.

Prayer: *Dear Lord, thank you for loving us. Please help us to remember Mary's trust and follow you in faith. Amen*

Thought for the day: With God, I can walk confidently into the unknown.

Bethany M-L Verrett (Virginia, USA)

Divine provision

Read Philippians 4:4–14

God will fully satisfy every need of yours according to his riches in glory in Christ Jesus.
Philippians 4:19 (NRSV)

We had been travelling all night in a bus. As we drove along, I sang a popular gospel song. Then, surprisingly, others joined in, singing in harmony. As we sang, we could see the trees on the sides of the road swaying left and right, as though clapping their hands in praise to God!

After more than 600 kilometres we arrived at Ikot Ekpene, a Nigerian town on the border of Cameroon, at 7.00 pm. As we got off the bus, suddenly I realised that I had no place to stay that night. However, before I could think of what to do next, a stranger walked up to me and said, 'Hello, man of God; you may come and spend the night in my home. I know God will bless me for that.' I sighed with relief. That night I was treated to a warm meal and a cosy room. The next day, I left for Cameroon, where I preached a sermon as a part of an evangelism mission.

When God calls us to serve, we can trust God to provide for us along our journey. Our gracious God will never leave us nor forsake us.

Prayer: *Eternal God, help us to obey you today, and grant us faith to see your provision. In Jesus' name. Amen*

Thought for the day: I can trust that God knows my needs.

Raphael Ufuoma Williams (Gauteng, South Africa)

Finishing the race

Read Isaiah 46:3–4

Being confident of this, that he who began a good work in you will carry it on to completion until the day of Christ Jesus.
Philippians 1:6 (NIV)

I'm ashamed to say I'm someone who often starts things with great enthusiasm but doesn't always finish them.

When a friend told me she was pregnant, I rushed out to buy some wool to crochet a cot blanket. By the time the baby was born I was about halfway through. Sadly, I then allowed myself to be distracted by other interests so that the almost-but-not-quite finished blanket was still sitting at the bottom of my sewing basket when my friend's son left home and moved abroad to start a new job!

My zest for new things often peters out like a damp squib. So, how was I to keep going beyond the first flush of enthusiasm when I became a Christian? Thankfully, I have come to realise that in committing my life to Jesus, the Son of God, I have placed myself in the hands of the supreme 'completer/finisher'.

Jesus, on our behalf, lived the perfect human life all the way through. At its end he could say, 'It is finished.' Now he is at work replacing our old self with his most perfect self. He is the master craftsman and we are his workmanship. He never gives up. So, now our trust is in him and not in our own stickability.

Prayer: *Dear Lord, thank you for drawing us to yourself. Please keep hold of us right to the end. Amen*

Thought for the day: God will never let me go.

Valerie Eker (England, United Kingdom)

The waiting room

Read 1 John 4:7–15

Dear friends, let us love one another, for love comes from God.
Everyone who loves has been born of God and knows God.
1 John 4:7 (NIV)

I was in the doctor's waiting room when a young man came in. After being greeted by the receptionist, he sat by me. His clothing, a factory uniform, was dirty, and he smelled of hard work. I smiled but wished he had sat somewhere else. After a moment, I recognised something familiar in his scent. It was the odour my father had when he came home from work at a similar factory.

My father was a faithful Christian. Perhaps this young man was a Christian. Maybe he loved to hug and kiss his children like my father did me. I was ashamed for judging my him negatively. I had forgotten the teachings of the good news: 'Dear friends, let us love one another, for love comes from God.'

God loves us all and shares life with us all. Jesus Christ was crucified and resurrected because God sent his Son into the world in the ultimate act of love. In Christ, no matter who we are or what we do, we are to care for and love one another as we love God and are loved by God.

Prayer: *Dear God, help us try to love everyone we meet as you love us. Amen*

Thought for the day: I will take the time to see each person I meet as a child of God.

Gordon Talk (Kentucky, USA)

Eyes on Jesus

Read Matthew 14:22–33

[The Lord] reached down from on high and took hold of me; he drew me out of deep waters.
Psalm 18:16 (NIV)

My mother died when I was in my 20s, so she never got to see and enjoy my five children. She was a doting grandmother (she already had 22 grandchildren), and she used to spend time with each of her daughters and daughters-in-law when they had their babies. She also knitted beautiful clothes for each one. She was always there for them.

I missed her particularly when we started our family, and I blamed God for taking her away when I needed her the most. For a while I focused more on the demands of parenting and my own constant weariness than I did on Jesus and his desire to walk with me through this season of doubt and grief.

In today's scripture reading, Peter took his eyes off Jesus too. He focused more on the storm around him than on the one who could calm the storm. Peter nearly drowned; but when he called out, Jesus saved him.

Storms in our lives can overwhelm us and may threaten to drown us in despair. But in those moments we can call out to Jesus, the one who can save us. Jesus cares more about the daily challenges of our lives than we may believe. We simply need to reach out to him in faith.

Prayer: *Thank you, Jesus, that you always hear our cries for help, no matter the time of day or night. Amen*

Thought for the day: Do I focus on the storm or the one who can calm the storm?

Dianne Fegan (Queensland, Australia)

True source

Read Colossians 1:9–14

I can do all things through [Christ] who strengthens me.
Philippians 4:13 (NRSV)

I took my mischievous Sheltie puppy, Misty, to obedience school to learn good manners. The dog trainer produced an astonishing change. The trainer's calm, kind demeanour impressed me, although I did not immediately understand why.

Sometime later while I was in hospital for shoulder surgery, I called the trainer and asked him to board Misty. When he brought Misty home, he told me he had visited my neighbours to ask if they would be willing to help me and had collected their contact information. Before he left, he gave me a copy of *The Upper Room*, explaining that his family read the devotional every day. I asked for his favourite Bible verse. Without hesitation, he said, 'I can do all things through him who strengthens me.' Suddenly I understood that faith was the source of his compassion.

The kindness of this dog trainer touched me deeply. His example of holiness is within the reach of all of us. Wherever we are, we can bear witness to God's loving-kindness and reveal God's good news through small gestures done with great love.

Prayer: *Loving Father, make us aware of your presence so that we may bear witness to your love in all that we do. Amen*

Thought for the day: God can use my ordinary actions of love to bring compassion to the world.

Janice Davin (North Carolina, USA)

I was a stranger

Read Matthew 25:34–40

'So in everything, do to others what you would have them do to you, for this sums up the Law and the Prophets.'
Matthew 7:12 (NIV)

Several years ago, the premises where the local Muslim community meets to socialise and worship was firebombed and required lengthy repairs. Their meeting place is in the parish for which our church has special responsibility. After due deliberation, and consultation with other local churches of various denominations, our church offered the Muslims temporary accommodation in a room on our church premises. They accepted.

Some Christians (both locally and nationally) did not approve of what we did. Some expressed their doubts, while a few were positively hostile. Others, however, especially members of the local churches, were outspoken in their support.

Why did we take the action we did? It was not an inter-faith act, but rather a simple adherence to the teachings of Jesus. Several gospel passages come to mind, including 'I was a stranger and you invited me in' and 'Do to others what you would have them do to you.'

Prayer: *Dear Lord, help us to show our love for you not only in our devotions but in our actions towards our neighbours. Amen*

Thought for the day: Who are the 'strangers' in my community that I can show the love of Jesus to?

William Findlay (Scotland, United Kingdom)

My unique role

Read 1 Corinthians 12:12–20

I praise you [Lord] because I am fearfully and wonderfully made.
Psalm 139:14 (NIV)

I enjoy walking around the block and taking in the many colours of the plants and flowers. It amazes me how effortlessly the flowers seem to blossom, each bringing their own uniqueness, splendour and contribution to the garden. Together the plants form a majestic oasis amid the pavement.

In taking time to notice the intricate details of God's creation, I realised that we all can learn from these wonderful plants. They come in different shapes, sizes, colours and fragrances, yet they don't compare or compete. They seem effortlessly content with how God has made them. I believe God intends for us to be this way as well.

God made each of us unique. When we embrace the way God made us and continues to shape us, we can stand with confidence, knowing that there will never be anyone exactly like us. Just as a garden needs many varieties of plants, the body of Christ needs many different members. We may not be perfect, but we are certainly precious. The more fully we believe that, the more God can use us as gifts and blessings to others.

Prayer: *Heavenly Father, help us to see our beauty and to avoid comparisons. Remind us to embrace our unique role in the world so that we may bless others. In Jesus' name. Amen*

Thought for the day: When I embrace who God created me to be, I can better serve God and others.

Gursimran Chhatwal (Haryana, India)

Reaching out

Read Luke 19:1–10

*When Jesus came to the place, he looked up and said to him,
'Zacchaeus, hurry and come down; for I must stay at your house
today.'*
Luke 19:5 (NRSV)

A few years ago my family and I were at Cambridge University around the
time of the annual examinations. As we walked, I saw a student sitting
alone on a bench with his head in his hands. I thought about going over
to comfort him, but I hesitated, conflicted. Then I walked on by. Could
I have made a difference by quietly supporting him in what appeared to
be a moment of crisis? I will never know, but I regret to this day not going
over to sit beside him.

There have been times in my life when I longed for someone to reach
out to me. A few weeks after the death of my mother, I was in morning
worship feeling sad. I yearned for someone to ask me if I was doing okay,
because at that moment I was not. I guess my game face fooled everyone
because no one asked.

Sometimes we hesitate to reach out to someone for fear of offend-
ing them. But by not doing so we also miss the chance to offer comfort and support to those who really want and need it. Time and again
Jesus reached out to others, offering healing and acceptance. Reaching
out to a hurting person is not easy for me, but I try, inspired by Jesus'
brave examples. I believe that the power of personal connection out-
weighs any risk.

Prayer: *Dear Jesus, encourage us when we hesitate to reach out to
those around us who are hurting or alone. Amen*

Thought for the day: Offering God's love and comfort to others is
worth the risk.

Donald Greeley (Illinois, USA)

Signs of God's faithfulness

I have an odd collection of objects that are very special to me – an empty aluminium package that once contained ground coffee, a small white rock, three golf tees, an inexpensive digital wristwatch that is scratched and discoloured. One might think that my collection is stuff that needs to be discarded, but each object holds memories for me of significant moments or time spent with people I love.

Many of these objects reside in a piece of pottery in my home. Often in passing I will pause, select one and hold it in my hand for a few seconds. I take a moment to dwell in the memory associated with the object before putting it back in its place. My collection contains some of my most valued possessions, not because they are worth much monetarily, but because they are so closely tied with rich memories and people who are important to me.

When I look through my collection, I am reminded of a story in which Samuel constructed a memorial after God saved the Israelites from the Philistines: 'Samuel took a stone and set it up between Mizpah and Shen. He named it Ebenezer, saying, "Thus far the Lord has helped us"' (1 Samuel 7:12, NIV). The purpose of the memorial was to remind the Israelites of God's help and faithfulness. I have come to think of each object in my collection as a kind of Ebenezer, a reminder of one of the many ways that God has been faithful to me – the gift of a good friend, time spent with family or time spent in solitude in nature, to name only a few.

This story from Samuel reminds me of the importance of recalling God's faithfulness in the past, because those memories can shape the present. When I remember God's help in the past, I am encouraged and sustained here and now, especially when God feels distant or silent.

I now have a regular discipline of keeping a running mental list of all the Ebenezers in my life. This has been particularly helpful in challenging times or when I'm just feeling burned out, bored or irritable. I take a moment to pause and recite all the things for which I am grateful – people in my life, fun and memorable experiences, whatever comes to mind.

I spend time dwelling in this mental collection in much the same way I do with the objects in my piece of pottery.

Often the beginning of a new year is a time to look forward, to set goals and make plans. But this year instead of only looking forward, I am going to be intentional about also looking back and reflecting on all the ways God has been faithful to me over the past year. I invite you to take some time to do the same. Whether you start a physical list or keep a mental one or begin your own collection of objects, my hope for you is that your life is replete with signs of God's faithfulness. I hope too that what has been true for me is also true for you – that the more you look for those signs, the more you are able to find.

QUESTIONS FOR REFLECTION

1   What practices or disciplines remind you of and help you reflect on God's faithfulness to you?

2   Why is it important that we remember the ways that God has been faithful to us? Name a time when remembering God's faithfulness has changed your attitude about a situation.

3   What other examples in scripture can you think of where a person or group made a memorial as a reminder of God's help?

Andrew Garland Breeden, acquisitions editor

Real courage

Read Joshua 1:1–9
Be strong and courageous.
Joshua 1:6 (NIV)

I was sitting alone in my small trailer home, reading a morning devotion. I couldn't go anywhere because of the threat of the Covid-19 pandemic. I was worried and a bit scared because I was also having strong allergy symptoms that had lasted a month. Could it be the virus, not allergies?

As I continued to read my devotions, I found that God had to tell Joshua – a strong, brave warrior – three times in nine verses not to be afraid but to be strong and courageous. Somehow those three repeated admonitions made me a little stronger and more courageous as well. They reminded me that God is watching over me too. Then another verse from Joshua's story rang clear to me: 'I will never leave you nor forsake you.' Those words were also meant for you and me.

The constant commentary in our news and social media can easily stir up fear and hopelessness. But we can counter that with God's words to Joshua, 'I will never leave you… Be strong and courageous.' Holding on to that promise, we can relax and do the things we must do, always with the knowledge that we are not alone; our God is watching over us. 'In peace I will lie down and sleep, for you alone, Lord, make me dwell in safety' (Psalm 4:8).

Prayer: *Forgive us, Father, when we forget that you are watching over us, even in a pandemic. Remove our fear, and renew our trust in you. Amen*

Thought for the day: Because God is for me, I will not give in to fear.

Ken Claar (Idaho, USA)

Walking the labyrinth

Read Matthew 11:25–30

Jesus answered, 'I am the way and the truth and the life.'
John 14:6 (NIV)

The stone was damp on my bare feet as I entered the labyrinth. Breeze, moist earth and birdsong stirred my senses as I walked my prayer in the enclosed garden of the retreat house.

Initially, the circuitous path drew close to the centre of the labyrinth, but it quickly veered away into a tangle of loops. I began to wonder if I was ever going to reach the centre. But, as in life, our paths are rarely straight. The secret, in the labyrinth, is to relax into a slow rhythm, becoming aware of the movements of the Spirit. Suddenly, you'll find yourself at the centre with space to reflect and be still.

The value of walking a labyrinth, like any pilgrimage, is not so much journeying to find God as walking with God in the moment. As I slowly placed one foot in front of the other, I could imagine Jesus patiently walking with me, inviting me to accept his gentle yoke for the journey ahead. What a reassuring message to bring back with me into my everyday life!

None of us knows where our paths are leading, but we can trust Jesus, our Saviour and friend, to guide us. He is our way.

Prayer: *Dear Jesus, place your yoke upon us, and help us to walk lightly with you today. Amen*

Thought for the day: When my path is confusing, I can trust that Jesus journeys with me.

April McIntyre (England, United Kingdom)

Angels of mercy

Read Philippians 2:1–11

Let each of you look not to your own interests, but to the interests of others. Let the same mind be in you that was in Christ Jesus.
Philippians 2:4–5 (NRSV)

For 33 years I suffered from kidney stones and often required hospitalisation for several days at a time. My doctors concluded the stones were caused by stress and suggested that I find ways to cope with my anxiety. 'That's more easily said than done,' I thought, as I considered my family, work and volunteer commitments.

However, a combination of prayer, meditation, nutrition and exercise have led to a healthy body. It's now been 10 years since I had my last kidney stone. As I reflect on this experience, I realise that much of my growth has been spiritual. During each recovery I had to rely completely on medical personnel, family and friends. As a result, I learned that God sends angels of mercy – the people who reflect God's love by sending cards, making calls, preparing food and praying. I have been richly blessed by these folks who seek to do good.

As today's reading reminds us, we are called to care for one another with the love of Christ. Perhaps this means seeking out someone who is sick or deployed or undergoing medical treatments or putting the pieces together after a divorce. In God's name, we are to actively love those who suffer.

Prayer: *God, our ultimate healer, thank you for calling us to serve as ministering angels of mercy to those in need. Give us the strength to love others with your love. Amen*

Thought for the day: I can be God's hands of help and healing for someone today.

Richard L. Whitaker (North Carolina, USA)

Keep sowing

Read Ecclesiastes 11:1–6

Many are the plans in a person's heart, but it is the Lord's purpose that prevails.
Proverbs 19:21 (NIV)

One morning while walking in town, I silently lamented to God about a painful rejection. A writing professional had not only given a negative critique of a story I had invested years crafting, they also advised me to walk away from the project. Tears rimmed my eyes. Was it time to give up writing for publication and find another way to honour God and bless others?

As I continued my walk, a piece of litter in the road caught my eye. Nestled against the curb was a half-full pack of pens. I picked it up and pulled out the two that remained. They were my favourite kind: black ink, bold strokes, comfortable grip. I smiled and thanked God for this gift. What others may have seen as trash, I now clutched as a tangible sign that I should keep writing.

Today's reading reminds us that we never know which of the seeds we sow in faith will blossom. God alone knows which ones will flourish and which ones will wither. Failure stings, yet we will not reap a harvest if we never risk planting. Scripture invites us to keep sowing because we can trust God with the results.

Prayer: *Faithful God, when we are discouraged at the lack of visible success, remind us that you will prevail and that our job is to continue to sow the seeds. Amen*

Thought for the day: By faith I will sow seeds and trust God with the harvest.

David Brannock (Tennessee, USA)

The good shepherd

Read Psalm 23:1–6

Even though I walk through the darkest valley, I will fear no evil, for you are with me.
Psalm 23:4 (NIV)

My doctor recently diagnosed me with a myoma, a non-cancerous tumour around my uterus. He gave me a round of medicines and asked me to come back when they ran out. I took my prescription and prayed, asking for prayers from my family in Christ as well.

I was sure I had recovered, but my check-up revealed that the myoma was still there. I was disappointed. But I felt God ask me, 'Lina, am I a good God?' I was speechless. After a few minutes I was able to answer, 'Yes. You are very good to me.'

I thought of David's words in Psalm 23. With God as my shepherd, I lack nothing. God makes me lie down in green pastures and leads me beside quiet waters.

But there are also moments of life, David acknowledges, where we walk through the darkest valley. And even in those times, we can fear no evil because God is with us and the darkness is not permanent. In today's reading, David does not ask, 'Why did you put me here?' when facing the darkness. Rather, David proclaims trust in his good shepherd. I too can proclaim trust. God is with me through all my challenges.

Prayer: *Good shepherd, thank you for walking with us. Because of you, we do not need to be afraid. Because of you, we can overcome all challenges. Amen*

Thought for the day: My situation may be challenging, but God is always good.

Linawati Santoso (East Java, Indonesia)

Made whole

Read Jeremiah 18:1–6

Heal me, Lord, and I shall be healed; save me and I shall be saved, for you are the one I praise.
Jeremiah 17:14 (NIV)

I dropped the Communion chalice! It slipped out of my hands and broke into pieces on the concrete. This special chalice, which I had borrowed, belonged to my church. What was I to do? I was almost sick with worry. So I gathered up the chalice pieces and took them to a local potter. He studied the shards for several moments, then looked me directly in the eyes and said, 'This is a broken mess, but I will see what I can do. Come back next week.'

When I returned the following week, I could not believe my eyes! The potter had taken my broken mess and transformed it into a whole chalice once again. Yes, fracture lines remained; but the cup was beautifully mended and functional once more. How appropriate, it seemed, that a chalice chosen to contain the fruit of the vine representing the blood of Christ now bears the marks and scars of repaired brokenness, reminding us that we too may be made whole.

We, like the chalice, have been broken and scarred. Yet, when we bring our broken, messy lives to God, we find forgiveness and restoration. God's amazing grace, exemplified through Christ, puts us back together so that we are forgiven, freed and empowered for fruitfulness in God's kingdom.

Prayer: *Gracious Lord, thank you that by your scars we are healed and made whole. Empower us to serve you each and every day. Amen*

Thought for the day: Christ chose to be broken so that we could be whole.

Michael D. Kurtz (North Carolina, USA)

Boundless love

Read Ephesians 2:4–10

Because of his great love for us, God, who is rich in mercy, made us alive with Christ even when we were dead in transgressions – it is by grace you have been saved.
Ephesians 2:4–5 (NIV)

I sat with my daughter on the beach. Close by, a young girl and boy played in the sand. The children bickered a little and the boy ran to their caretaker yelling, 'She's using up all the sand!' My daughter and I stifled giggles at the statement as we surveyed the expansive sandy beach around us.

But as I reflected on this child's statement, I realised that I have had thoughts just as absurd. During a dark time in my life, I once believed my poor choices and sin had exhausted God's love for me. I struggled to believe otherwise. In time, I learned God's love is limitless, more vast than even the sands on this beach.

The psalmist was so overcome with God's boundless love that he repeats 26 times 'His love endures forever' in Psalm 136. God's love has no limit or expiration date. It will not fail or diminish. I am so grateful we can never use it up.

Prayer: *Dear Lord, thank you for your limitless love, which you demonstrated through Jesus who died for us. Help us live in a way that others may know your love as we pray, 'Father, hallowed be your name, your kingdom come. Give us each day our daily bread. Forgive us our sins, for we also forgive everyone who sins against us. And lead us not into temptation.'* Amen*

Thought for the day: I can trust that God's love for me will never end.

Beverly Varnado (Georgia, USA)

Metamorphosis

Read John 16:25–33

*'I have told you these things, so that in me you may have peace.
In this world you will have trouble. But take heart! I have overcome
the world.'*
John 16:33 (NIV)

I taught first grade for more than 30 years. One day, one of my students
brought a caterpillar to the classroom. We placed it in a glass jar, along
with some leaves and dried twigs. For several days, we watched the
caterpillar. One morning, the children were upset because the caterpillar was gone. Instead, resting on a dry twig was a prepupa. I took
that moment to explain the metamorphosis: the prepupa hardens to
form a chrysalis and inside the chrysalis, the pupa changes into an adult
butterfly. The students kept watch for almost two weeks, but there was
no apparent change.

Then one day, a student pointed excitedly towards the glass jar,
saying, 'It's moving!' The students gathered round to observe as a weak
butterfly struggled to break through. It was hard work; the progress,
difficult. I explained to the students that the difficult struggle is what
strengthens its legs and wings so that it can fly.

In a similar way, the preparation for our metamorphosis lies in the
struggles and pain that strengthen our faith. God is in our every struggle,
working with us and for us. And with God's help, we will take flight
because God always works for our good.

Prayer: *Creator God, we thank you for your constant presence –
a loving reminder that you work within us in our struggles to help us
grow and remain strong. Amen*

Thought for the day: The struggles I face can make me stronger and
draw me closer to God.

Zobeida Carrasquillo (Puerto Rico)

Anytime, anywhere

Read James 5:13–18

This is the confidence we have in approaching God: that if we ask anything according to his will, he hears us.
1 John 5:14 (NIV)

When I was a child, I spent a part of each summer with my grandparents. I loved exploring around their big farm. One day as I was going down to the creek to rake out pretty rocks, I heard my grandpa praying. His voice was coming from the corn crib where he often had his private devotions. As I listened, I heard him call my name. Grandpa asked God to put a desire in my heart to live for God and for God to keep me safe from harm. I never forgot that prayer. I wondered if he prayed for me daily. Somehow that thought made me feel safe and secure.

When I was a teenager, I gave my heart to the Lord and have tried to be a faithful Christ-follower for many years. I now pray daily for my six grandchildren.

The Bible tells us that 'the prayer of a righteous person is powerful and effective' (James 5:16). My grandpa's prayers for me have taught me that we can pray for anyone, anytime, anywhere: members of our family, the children at the nearby park or playground, a stranger on the bus. Then, in Psalm 91:15 we can find assurance that God hears and answers us: 'When they call to me, I will answer them; I will be with them in trouble, I will rescue them and honour them' (NRSV).

Prayer: *O God, thank you for the people who pray for us and the positive influence they can have on our lives. Amen*

Thought for the day: Today I will pray for the people I see around me.

Frankie Roland (Colorado, USA)

Not bothering God

Read Luke 8:49–56

*While Jesus was still speaking, someone came from the house of
Jairus, the synagogue leader. 'Your daughter is dead,' he said. 'Don't
bother the teacher anymore.' Hearing this, Jesus said to Jairus, 'Don't
be afraid; just believe, and she will be healed.'*
Luke 8:49–50 (NIV)

My son placed frozen waffles into the toaster, and while he watched his
favourite food toast, I cooked eggs. Suddenly, he screamed. I whirled
around to see red fingers and teary eyes. As he pulled a waffle from the
toaster, he had burned his fingers on the heating element. 'I didn't want
to bother you,' he said, crying. After bandaging his fingers and serving up
his waffle with extra butter and syrup, I assured him that he can always
ask me for help, no matter what.

Similarly, it's easy for me to believe that my problems are too small
for God to care about or that God is too busy to answer my prayers. Like
Jairus' companion in Luke 8, my immediate circumstances, friends or
family often dissuade me from bringing my concerns to the Lord. I try to
fix my addictions, failures and broken relationships on my own, and my
heart ends up needlessly wounded.

Yet God's love persistently calls to me, reminding me not to be afraid
and to trust God's wisdom. Just as parents delight in helping their children, so God delights in helping us. I can tell and ask God anything. God
isn't bothered by my pleas, and asking builds my faith. God's provisions
spur my gratitude and praise.

Prayer: *Dear God, thank you for caring about every detail of our lives
and for always being ready to help us in our times of need. Amen*

Thought for the day: Through prayer and praise I can share my daily
life with God.

Kathleen Elizabeth Dunlap (Colorado, USA)

What's inside

Read 1 Samuel 16:1–13

The Lord said unto Samuel, Look not on his countenance, or on the height of his stature; because I have refused him: for the Lord seeth not as man seeth; for man looketh on the outward appearance, but the Lord looketh on the heart.
1 Samuel 16:7 (KJV)

When I was in university, I was given cans of milk to take to school. I took care to clean the cans regularly and kept them in a secure place, but I didn't consume the milk for several months. I thought that if the cans were clean and attractive on the outside, the milk inside would be okay. However, when I eventually opened one of the cans, I was surprised to see that the milk had expired and turned sour. Though outwardly the cans looked fine, the contents were unattractive and unusable.

Many times we take care of our outward appearance, ensuring that we look good. Yet we less frequently turn our attention inward. Many times we leave our hearts filled with malice, envy, grudges, deceit or pride instead of love. Even when our outward appearance is beautiful, our hearts may not be.

God is concerned with what is inward. God wants us to have loving and forgiving hearts. David's brothers appeared good from the outside, but God rejected them because of their hearts. We please God when we look inward and care for our hearts as much as we care for our outward appearance.

Prayer: *Dear God, create in us a right spirit. Help us to see the harmful things we harbour in our hearts and to let them go. Amen*

Thought for the day: God cares about my heart more than my outward appearance.

Olajide Kazeem Olatunji (Oyo State, Nigeria)

Unity in Christ

Read John 17:17–26

'I pray they will be one, Father, just as you are in me and I am in you. I pray that they also will be in us, so that the world will believe that you sent me.'
John 17:21 (CEB)

Seeing a huge, disorganised group of ducks flying overhead, I pulled to the side of the road to get a better look. I witnessed three groups merge into a giant V formation. The newly formed flock then stayed together, at times changing positions but keeping in formation. When one bird fell behind, two others fell back with it until they were able to rejoin the group and return to their original positions. What a sight to behold!

This kind of unity doesn't always come so naturally for brothers and sisters in Christ. But imagine what could be accomplished if every member of God's flock embraced their role, knowing that everyone is critical to the success of the flock arriving at its destination. Imagine if all joined in unity, striving and surrendering themselves to God's purpose.

Being in unity isn't just possible; it's God's desire and plan. Jesus prayed for his disciples to be one as Jesus and his Father were one and later sent the Holy Spirit to empower and bond us. God wants us to embrace our place in the flock. If brothers or sisters in Christ fall behind, God calls us to help restore them to their place.

When Christians lay aside differences and focus on being one in Christ, working together for God's purpose, the possibilities are endless!

Prayer: *Father God, help us to walk in unity with our brothers and sisters in Christ. Amen*

Thought for the day: God desires for me to walk in unity with other Christians.

Therese Marszalek (Minnesota, USA)

Always in God's presence

Read Psalm 139:13–18
If I go up to the heavens, you are there; if I make my bed in the depths, you are there.
Psalm 139:8 (NIV)

About 20 years ago I suffered with a prolonged illness that severely limited my life. I spent most of my time in bed or in a chair. I felt horrible and fell into a deep depression.

One Saturday morning I was talking with my wife as she patiently listened to my fear and hopelessness. 'I feel as if God has abandoned me,' I cried. 'My head is telling me that it isn't true, but the feelings seem so convincing.'

'Why don't you call your friend Michael?' she asked. 'You encourage each other when you're down; and I bet he'd like to hear from you.'

Later that day I did call Michael. 'Gary!' he said excitedly. 'I was walking on the beach this morning, and the Lord put a new song in my heart. I think it's for you.' Then he sang it to me: 'I'm always in your presence, I'm always under your watchful eye. I'm always in your presence, even though these feelings would lie.'

'Michael,' I said, 'you have no idea how much that means to me.' Then I told him about my conversation with my wife and about my illness. Michael said, 'That's how much God loves you, mate! While you were talking with your wife, the Lord was giving me a song just for you.'

That day became a powerful reminder: I have always been in the presence of the Lord!

Prayer: *Thank you, Lord, for watching over us and never letting us out of your sight. Help us to remember that you will bring us peace in our struggles. Amen*

Thought for the day: When I feel abandoned by God, I can turn to faithful friends for reassurance.

Gerard Eha (Florida, USA)

PRAYER FOCUS: THOSE WHO FEEL ABANDONED BY GOD

Smoothing out

Read Galatians 5:22–25

If anyone is in Christ, there is a new creation: everything old has passed away; see, everything has become new!
2 Corinthians 5:17 (NRSV)

One day I decided to turn my small pieces of leftover soap bars into one big bar of soap that would be usable. I cut the pieces smaller and melted them down, and then I worked to mould the soap into a usable shape. Eventually it seemed to be nice and round, but after letting it dry for 24 hours, many lumps and bumps became visible. However, as I use the soap, the bumps are slowly smoothing out and the soap is becoming more rounded and easier to use.

This reminds me of how the Holy Spirit works with me, a flawed human being. Patiently the Holy Spirit works to smooth out all the parts of me that are not glorifying to God – a lifelong process that ensures that I continue to serve God in meaningful ways.

Sometimes this process can be painful or drawn out, but I know that God knows what is best. I only have to be willing to let the Holy Spirit shape me to be more like Jesus Christ.

Prayer: *Loving God, help us to embrace your shaping of us so that we can show your love, patience and long-suffering to others. Amen*

Thought for the day: Every time I wash today, I will remember God's great love for me.

Christine Hay (Scotland, United Kingdom)

Alive and active

Read Matthew 14:22–33

The word of God is living and active, sharper than any two-edged sword, piercing until it divides soul from spirit, joints from marrow; it is able to judge the thoughts and intentions of the heart.
Hebrews 4:12 (NRSV)

I took my family to see a musical. After it was over, I asked everyone what they liked most about it. My daughter, who plays piano, said that she liked the songs the best. My other daughter, who likes to read, was intrigued by the story. My wife, who is a people person, enjoyed watching how the audience reacted to what was happening. They all saw the same musical, but they each were affected by a different aspect of it.

The same is true of the Bible. The Holy Spirit can take any story and speak different things to us depending on what we need to hear at the time. Matthew 14:22–33 is the story of Jesus, and then Peter, walking on the sea. Someone who is going through trials may see how Jesus comes to us in our distress. Someone who is struggling with doubt may see how Peter did something extraordinary by simply trusting Jesus. And someone who is wondering about prayer may see the effectiveness of Peter's prayer, 'Lord, save me!'

When we read and study the Bible, it is amazing how personal the word of God can be. Through scripture, God speaks to our individual hearts and tells us what we need to hear.

Prayer: *Holy Spirit, create in our hearts a desire to read the Bible and get to know you. Speak to us in our study that we may be inspired, challenged and transformed. Amen*

Thought for the day: When I read the Bible, God meets me in the word.

Bob LaForge (New Jersey, USA)

What no longer works

Read 2 Corinthians 5:16–21

'No one pours new wine into old wineskins. Otherwise, the wine will burst the skins, and both the wine and the wineskins will be ruined. No, they pour new wine into new wineskins.'
Mark 2:22 (NIV)

It had been a year since I last made apple sauce from fresh apples. I was eager to get into the task and gathered my tools quickly. As I started to prepare the apples for cooking, I was struggling to core them. Then I remembered I had bought a new apple corer – yet I was still struggling with the old, dull one. Why had I not simply discarded the old one that no longer worked well?

It can be like that in my spiritual life too. I cling to old routines and old habits that no longer serve me well. As today's passage from 2 Corinthians tells us, in Christ we are new – the old is gone.

I make life more difficult when I refuse to part with what no longer works, forgetting to seek God's guidance and use the new ways that God gives me. Reading scripture from a new perspective and discussing what I read with other Christians helps. And always, we can pray, asking God for enlightenment and guidance.

Prayer: *Loving God, help us to discard our old ways and remain open to new experiences and fresh perspectives that bring us closer to you. Amen*

Thought for the day: When I let go of what no longer serves me, God will guide me to fresh ways.

April Bogert (New York, USA)

Aroma of Christ

Read 2 Corinthians 2:14–17

We are to God the pleasing aroma of Christ among those who are being saved and those who are perishing.
2 Corinthians 2:15 (NIV)

On my way to church one Sunday morning, I noticed a pleasant scent. I looked up and saw olive flowers in bloom. Each of the small flowers was giving off a gentle aroma. The scent lifted my spirits, and I thanked God for the wonders of creation.

The fragrance reminded me of the passage from 2 Corinthians above. I have met some people who spread the aroma of Christ and have felt the presence of God in their ministries. I always hope to be like them, but I'm uncertain about my ability to do so.

However, I felt the Lord reassure me through those olive flowers that I should not compare myself to others. Olive blossoms are smaller in size than roses and their blooming season is different from other flowers. But in the season and the manner that God designed for them, they spread an aroma that tells us of God's wonderful creation. Furthermore, I need not rely on my own abilities, for it is God who created me. Like the olive flowers that bloom and spread their aroma naturally, God will enable me to spread an aroma of faith.

Prayer: *God of creation, thank you for your love. Use each of us as your vessels to fill this world with the aroma of Christ's presence. Amen*

Thought for the day: God will help me to share the good news in my own unique way.

Hisako Adachi (Kanagawa, Japan)

Beginning to heal

Read Psalm 119:25–32

All scripture is inspired by God and is useful for teaching, for reproof, for correction, and for training in righteousness, so that everyone who belongs to God may be proficient, equipped for every good work.
2 Timothy 3:16–17 (NRSV)

'How could someone in his 30s have this much back pain?' I wondered. One day the pain just showed up. I didn't know what had caused it, but it hurt all day and night – as I sat to do my work, while standing to cook dinner, when working outside in the yard and while trying to sleep at night. I went to the doctor, but even after months of X-rays, consultations, referrals, physical therapy and medication, nothing had helped.

I resolved to try something new: I would walk 30 minutes a day for 30 days. After walking daily for a week, the pain had lessened. The following two weeks, the pain was even less. And after one month of daily walks, my back felt better than it had in a year. The regular, gentle exercise was helping to heal my back, loosen the muscles and eliminate my pain.

Everyone has pain at some point. Often the pain we feel most is emotional, be it from unkind words, betrayal or grief. When we are in emotional pain, spending time with God begins to heal us. Even spending 30 minutes a day reading God's word will help reduce our pain. Just as walking every day healed my back, reading God's word every day heals our hearts.

Prayer: *Dear God, thank you for giving us your word. Help us make time to meditate on it daily. Amen*

Thought for the day: God's word helps me to heal and live fully.

Christopher L. Scott (Washington, USA)

What's my motivation?

Read Matthew 6:1–4

'Be careful not to practice your righteousness in front of others to be seen by them. If you do, you will have no reward from your Father in heaven.'
Matthew 6:1 (NIV)

During an extended holiday with my husband, I received an alert on my phone from our home security system. I checked the cameras and was surprised to see our son mowing the lawn. He is a busy law student, and we had not seen him much lately. I was not sure he even knew we were on holiday. I quickly sent him a text message thanking him. He responded, 'You can quit spying on me now. I forgot about the cameras. Now my surprise is spoiled.'

This led me to consider my own motivations for doing good deeds. I have always been active in church mission projects and philanthropic endeavours. Did I do them privately with the sole intent of helping others, or did I do them for public acknowledgement of my goodness? My son's intended surprise was for the right reasons, and I was humbled by the lesson it taught me. God wants our motivation to be pure, sincere and selfless. Even if our good deeds are known only to God and ourselves, when we know we care for others out of the love in our hearts, that is the only reward we need.

Prayer: *Dear Lord, help us remain motivated by compassion and love for others and not our own desire for admiration and praise. Amen*

Thought for the day: Doing good deeds is rewarding, no matter who knows of my actions.

Pamela Briese (Iowa, USA)

First days

Read Genesis 1:1–5

God said, 'Let there be light,' and there was light.
Genesis 1:3 (NIV)

The first day of a new venture can be both exciting and unnerving. My first day of college brought many firsts – a new job, a new city, a new church, a new home. These firsts brought a mix of anticipation and apprehension into my life.

With each new venture, I know what I am leaving behind, but I don't know what I will find ahead. This requires me to learn to trust God over again – I know of God's past faithfulness, but I have to overcome my apprehension about the future.

Recently I retired and struggled with a new first – trying to find my place in a new season of life. Thankfully, God knows all about first days – after all God created them! When God created the world, God created light out of darkness and called light 'day' and darkness 'night.' Each day brought a new beginning and ending, and each new day God is faithful in giving us light.

As we face new beginnings and an unknown future, we can take heart because God is with us. We can trust God to guide us and provide for our needs. God leads, encourages and supports us through all of our days and has promised never to leave or forsake us (see Deuteronomy 31:6).

Prayer: *Dear Lord, remind us that you go before us this day. Let the light of your word lead and guide us in whatever we may face. Amen*

Thought for the day: God is with me in all my beginnings and endings.

Deborah Manera (Ontario, Canada)

Plastic bread bags

Read 1 Peter 2:4–10

See what great love the Father has lavished on us, that we should be called children of God! And that is what we are! The reason the world does not know us is that it did not know him.
1 John 3:1 (NIV)

One snowy, wet morning, my sister and I searched the kitchen for discarded bread bags. After the recent deaths of our parents, we couldn't afford decent footwear. Instead, we used bread bags to cover our socks so our feet and ankles would remain dry on the long walk to school. Upon arriving at school, I immediately went to the restroom and hid in a stall. Filled with shame, I removed the bread bags so nobody would see them and mock or bully me. I thought, 'I'm nothing but a worthless orphan. I'm rubbish, just like these bread bags.'

Since then, today's verse has taught me that I am not worthless. Rather, I'm greater than I could ever imagine because of God's boundless grace. I have been called and chosen to be an ambassador and steward and to bring God glory (see 2 Corinthians 5:17–21).

At times we may feel inferior or worthless, but God reminds us through scripture that we are mighty and of great value to God. We are not destined to be discarded as rubbish. We are sons and daughters of Almighty God. What a mind-boggling gift and honour!

Prayer: *Abba Father, when we feel inferior and worthless, please instil in our hearts the immense value and love you place on us. Amen*

Thought for the day: Today I will see myself as God sees me – worthy, holy and anointed.

Jim Good (Ohio, USA)

God's ways, not mine

Read Proverbs 3:5–8

*'My thoughts are not your thoughts, neither are your ways my ways,'
declares the Lord.*
Isaiah 55:8 (NIV)

In spring 2020, my husband and I were taking care of our dog, Kohl, after he had broken some vertebrae. Kohl was only ten months old and usually had lots of energy. But his injury had forced him to lie still in a confined area inside our garage for weeks. As I took care of him each day, I listened to his whines; I saw the sadness in his eyes and the urge he felt to break out of his cage and run free. But I knew if Kohl were let out of confinement, he could further injure himself, even so badly that he could become paralysed.

As I reflected on this situation, I thought of our great caretaker, God. I thought about how sometimes my life seemed bleak and discouraging; I didn't trust that God had a good plan for me. I had forgotten to 'lean not on [my] own understanding.'

When we feel restricted in life, it could be because our minds are limited. But God's ways are limitless. I have found my hope for living in trusting that God's plan for me is full of goodness, love and a joyful future. If I ever begin to doubt that promise, I have only to read the Bible and spend time with God in prayer.

Prayer: *Dear heavenly Father, forgive us when we doubt your goodness to us. Remind us of your loving ways that bring us joy in living. Move us to live in service to others. Amen*

Thought for the day: God has a good plan for me.

Stefan Woolsey-Lyons (Arkansas, USA)

The great commission

Read Matthew 28:16–20

'Go and make disciples of all nations, baptising them in the name of the Father and of the Son and of the Holy Spirit.'
Matthew 28:19 (NIV)

Every year I return to my family's beach house for a time of rest and relaxation. While there, I visit the park where my family and friends planted trees years ago. What completes the scene are the natural inhabitants of this area – ovenbirds, woodpeckers and larks.

Early one morning, I noticed the larks flying down to the park with their chicks to teach them to find food. Each day for several weeks, I observed the larks searching the grass for insects while their chicks chirped, eager to be fed. Under the watchful eye of the parents, the chicks gradually ventured farther and farther away.

While watching these birds, I saw a similarity with my faith journey. Early in my journey, I relied on more mature believers to teach me the word of God. Over time I learned the importance of prayer and maintaining a strong bond with God. Even as I continue to grow in my faith, I wonder: 'Do I move forward, confidently taking flight to carry the message of salvation to others? Or do I remain close to the nest because I am not ready to take flight?'

God calls us to active discipleship and to preach the gospel to all creation. With God's help, we can answer this call.

Prayer: *God of creation, grant us the wisdom and strength to grow in our faith and become more like Jesus, earnest in sharing the gospel with others. Amen*

Thought for the day: I can take flight in my faith journey because I know God is by my side.

Ana M. Buela (Buenos Aires, Argentina)

An answer to prayer

Read 2 Samuel 22:31–37

'It is God who arms me with strength and keeps my way secure.'
2 Samuel 22:33 (NIV)

I awoke with a feeling of dread. I was going to see our son in a nursing home for people with mental illness. The previous time my wife and I had visited was a disaster. Our son was combative, and his delusions were so strong that we weren't able to connect with him.

Now I was preparing to visit again, and I felt very apprehensive. As I do every morning, I read *The Upper Room* before I left. The writer spoke of heavy burdens and how God had met her every need, providing strength and rest. Reflecting on her words, I prayed for God to give me peace, patience and understanding for my upcoming visit. Immediately, I felt God's precious love surrounding me.

When I arrived, our son met me with a smile and big hug. The visit was the most fulfilling in years. His delusions were minimal. We spent time recalling happy memories. I was able to hear his great big belly laugh. When it was time to leave, he gave me another big hug.

How do I explain the gift of this visit? Was it just a coincidence? No! Our time together was an answer to prayer. Even in the midst of anxiety and difficult circumstances, God strengthens us with love and blesses us in unexpected, generous ways.

Prayer: *Loving God, help us always to put our trust in you when we are anxious. Thank you for giving us peace in our times of need and blessing us with moments of joy. Amen*

Thought for the day: God blesses me with unexpected gifts.

Bob Baer (Kansas, USA)

Planting seeds of faith

Read 1 Corinthians 3:5–11

I am sending [my dear brother and minister in the Lord] to you for this very purpose, to let you know how we are, and to encourage your hearts.
Ephesians 6:22 (NRSV)

I am a music leader for a Christian camp that serves adults with developmental disabilities. We plan worship services that incorporate musical arrangements of scripture with motions so that our nonverbal participants can better relate to God's word. At first I wondered if teaching scripture this way resonated with the campers.

Then one day, while walking through the centre of camp, I saw a camper named Josh walking towards me. He was humming to himself. When he saw me his face lit up, and he made the hand motions of the song we had sung that morning. In that moment, joy bubbled up inside me and with tears in my eyes I joined in with his song. We hugged, and he went on his way.

Scripture is not always accessible to people. That's why it is so important to me that we find ways to share scripture in many forms so that we can let God's words do the work of loving and reaching hearts. This experience gave me gratitude for the gift God has given me that enables me to tie music to scripture as a mnemonic device for all.

When we struggle to know if what we do in Christ's name is effective or if it even matters, we can ask God and trust that we will know – if not now, then in heaven.

Prayer: *Dear God, help us to share your word with everyone around us, especially those who don't often have the opportunity to access it. Amen*

Thought for the day: My efforts to share God's word are never in vain.

Laurie Hess Manzer (New York, USA)

Immersed in God

Read Psalm 139:1–10

Search me, O God, and know my heart; test me and know my thoughts.
Psalm 139:23 (NRSV)

Deep under Duke University in North Carolina lies a world filled with fluorescent-lit rooms and millions of books. I once spent a few afternoons working in this underground library. I was drawn more and more deeply into my research: from this book, to this author, to this journal. It was a completely immersive experience.

As Christians, we seek a similar type of captivation in our relationship with God. While God is ultimately beyond our understanding, our creator invites us in to learn about the Divine. We experience God through friendships, scripture, conversations and all that comes with them.

Psalm 139 reminds us that this deep searching can be reciprocal. Not only do we have the opportunity to explore God, but God desires to search our hearts. God loves us and wants to be immersed in our hearts and minds. While the Almighty can do anything, God first wants our permission for this relationship. God desires an invitation.

When we invite God in and take part in this mutual searching, we are transformed. In experiencing God and opening ourselves to the creator, we embrace our identity as the forgiven and become free to extend love, joy and compassion.

Prayer: *God of wisdom, thank you for allowing us to experience you. Help us to open our hearts to your Spirit that we may be forever changed. Amen*

Thought for the day: God desires to know me completely.

Ted Witham (Western Australia, Australia)

Mothering Sunday

Read Ephesians 4:11–16

I have no greater joy than to hear that my children are walking in the truth.
3 John 4 (NIV)

On Mothering Sunday, I always receive a card and gift from a younger friend who calls me her spiritual mum. I was surprised when she began to do this because she had become a Christian before I first met her. When I asked her about it, she replied, 'Yes, but you were the one who nurtured me, and that's the essential role of a mother after a child is born.'

This is the role that Jesus gave his followers before his ascension – to make disciples (see Matthew 28:19–20). Discipling is a step-by-step process of nurturing and training the new life that has been born, so that 'baby' Christians 'become mature' in the faith and in obedience to Christ Jesus. It requires prayer, teaching, giving support and encouragement, and leading by example.

My friend is now a mature Christian serving the Lord faithfully, and it has been a joy through many years to see how she has grown and uses her God-given gifts to the full.

Prayer: *Lord Jesus, let our lives and our words help new Christians grow in their love, faith and obedience to you. Amen*

Thought for the day: Who has been a spiritual parent to me?

Hazel V. Thompson (England, United Kingdom)

Reflect love

Read Ephesians 5:1–11

Follow God's example, therefore, as dearly loved children and live a life of love, just as Christ loved us and gave himself up for us as a fragrant offering and sacrifice to God.
Ephesians 5:1–2 (NIV)

Celebrities often get the spotlight, both for their achievements and their personal lives. They are like the stars in the sky or a town on a hill – clearly visible and guaranteed to attract attention.

However, because Christians are a minority group in my country, our presence is often noticed too. Whether at school, in the office or by our neighbours, people know Christ's teachings about love and observe whether Christians also reflect love in their words and deeds.

I feel that at times it can be difficult to reflect love because people are not always pleasant and my days are not always beautiful. But through daily reading of scripture, I am reminded that my words and deeds can determine whether or not God's name will be praised and glorified by those around me.

Prayer: *God Almighty, help us reflect your love to others so that our words and deeds glorify you. As Jesus taught us, we pray, 'Our Father which art in heaven, Hallowed be thy name. Thy kingdom come. Thy will be done in earth, as it is in heaven. Give us this day our daily bread. And forgive us our debts, as we forgive our debtors. And lead us not into temptation, but deliver us from evil: For thine is the kingdom, and the power, and the glory, forever.'* Amen*

Thought for the day: I can glorify God through my actions today.

Juita Kartini (Jakarta, Indonesia)

20/20 vision

Read Psalm 16:5–11

'The eye is the lamp of the body. So, if your eye is healthy, your whole body will be full of light.'
Matthew 6:22 (NRSV)

In the Covid-19 world of social distancing, officers at our prison have gotten creative in the games they devise for inmates. The latest contest involved competitive vision tests. I was happy to learn the winner was an inmate in my cellblock.

I went to congratulate him and noticed he was sad. He told me of his eagerness to be released and see his family. To my surprise, he opened up about his life and the events that had led him here. I asked him to join me in a prayer. When we finished, I encouraged him to take heart in the words of Revelation 3:20: 'Here I am! I stand at the door and knock. If anyone hears my voice and opens the door, I will come in.' I invited him to the worship service in the chapel that evening.

Back in my cell, I paused to reflect. My neighbour reminded me that we can be blessed with 20/20 eyesight and still fail to 'see' the obstacles that keep us from God. Luckily, God is steadfast and patient. When we place our trust in our Saviour, the Holy Spirit opens our spiritual eyes to see the path that God has laid before us, always leading towards our good.

Prayer: *All-knowing God, give us eyes to see you clearly and the people you have given us to love. Empower us, Holy Spirit, that we may be faithful and encourage others. Amen*

Thought for the day: When the way forward is unclear, God can open my eyes to hope.

Carlos Vázquez (Florida, USA)

What am I showcasing?

Read Ephesians 6:10–17

Be strong in the Lord and in the strength of his power.
Ephesians 6:10 (NRSV)

I have a terrace garden with a lot of potted plants. Each plant blooms in its own season. We all like to see beautiful things, so we showcase the best of what we have. I am always moving my plants around so that those with blooming flowers are visible. Those with no flowers are kept aside, though not discarded because God has a season for everything to be beautiful.

The seasons of our lives often bring their own kind of dormancy – situations and circumstances that are not very pretty. What do we do then? When we pass through such difficult times, what do we showcase? Is it our difficulties, or the strength of the Lord backing us up? Jesus promises in scripture never to leave or forsake us.

Our perspective matters. Focusing on the security God offers rather than our struggle brings beauty to an otherwise ugly situation. While we will sometimes falter as we seek God's strength, it's not about losing strength; it's about trusting that God has the power to revive us – again and again. Let's showcase the strength of God's Spirit so that the Spirit is able to bring renewed life in and through us.

Prayer: *Dear Lord, give us your strength so that we remain grounded in you. Live in us so that we can show your beauty and love to the world. In Jesus' name. Amen*

Thought for the day: In difficult times, I will stay focused on the strength of the Lord.

Deepika Emmanuel Sagar (Rajasthan, India)

Family reunited

Read Genesis 45:1–15

*A father to the fatherless, a defender of widows, is God in his holy
dwelling. God sets the lonely in families.*
Psalm 68:5–6 (NIV)

Recently I have been watching a television programme which seeks to
reunite parents and children who have been separated by adoption.
Many of the people break down in tears when reunited, and they often
say that an empty hole inside them is filled when they discover they are
still loved and not forgotten. Their family bond remains strong.

Such emotional scenes remind me of the story of Joseph's reunion
with his brothers. I love the moment when Joseph can no longer contain
himself and reveals his identity to his brothers. He weeps loudly and
reassures his brothers, who had years earlier sold him into slavery, to
not be distressed – God was at work. Later, Joseph was also reunited
with his father, Jacob.

But what about those who remain estranged? An adopted friend of
mine had traced her biological mother, but her mother wanted no contact. As a Christian, my friend was comforted by knowing that she is God's
beloved child. The quoted verse above reminds her that God is 'a father
to the fatherless' and 'sets the lonely in families', like her adoptive family.

Prayer: *Heavenly Father, thank you that you set the lonely in families.
Help those who are separated from their loved ones by illness, famine
or war. Amen*

Thought for the day: Through faith in Jesus, I am a child of God.

Faith Ford (England, United Kingdom)

Beloved children

Read Psalm 8

[The Lord] determines the number of the stars and calls them each by name.
Psalm 147:4 (NIV)

While looking through a book on astronomy, I came across a photo of a cluster of galaxies taken through a telescope. A cluster of *galaxies*! The realisation of that magnitude was so profound for me that I actually felt a headache.

The Milky Way galaxy resides among approximately one hundred thousand other galaxies in a supercluster named Laniakea. And Earth is located an estimated twenty-six thousand light-years from the centre of the Milky Way. There are not words sufficient to express the incredible size of the universe. How inexpressibly marvellous and enormous, then, is our God!

The psalmist's declaration that God determines the number of stars and gives them each a name could make some of us feel insignificant and small. Yet, in that complicated immensity, God chose to create us. God knows our names and abides in our hearts. Through our tears, laughter and experiences, God reaches out to us and names us Beloved Children. Praise be to God!

Prayer: *All-powerful and loving God, thank you for caring for each part of your creation and for calling us your children. Amen*

Thought for the day: Even though I am just a small part of the universe, God cares deeply for me.

Carrie Knight Kitzmiller (Texas, USA)

Consistent prayer

Read Luke 8:43–48

'Daughter, your faith has healed you,' Jesus said. 'Go in peace.'
Luke 8:48 (CEB)

I read today's passage of scripture from Luke 8 on the day before my surgery to remove a cancerous lump from my breast. Verse 48 spoke to me personally in several ways. Jesus called the woman 'Daughter,' which reminded me that I am a child of God and that our relationship is special. The words, 'Your faith has healed you,' also stood out to me. From the time I discovered the lump, during the numerous scans and tests, I prayed fervently and was aware of God's presence every step of the way. Many friends and family also prayed in faith for my healing. I was greatly comforted and touched by everyone's prayers which, as James 5:16 assures us, are powerful and effective. While reading Jesus' words, 'Go in peace,' I was at peace knowing that God was watching over me.

Luke 8:48 allowed me to be confident that whatever the outcome of my surgery, I was in God's hands. Thankfully, the outcome of my operation was better than I hoped. There was no cancer in my lymph nodes or anywhere else in my body. And although I need radiotherapy, I don't have to undergo chemotherapy. Praise the Lord!

Prayer: *Thank you, gracious Lord, that you are always with us in our struggles. Help us to place our trust in your loving care. Amen*

Thought for the day: When I pray, I become more aware of God's presence and grace.

Maree de Wet (KwaZulu-Natal, South Africa)

Music to my heart

Read Genesis 28:10–16

The Lord your God is in your midst – a warrior bringing victory. He will create calm with his love; he will rejoice over you with singing.
Zephaniah 3:17 (CEB)

Recently at church the praise team performed a beautiful song, and I began singing along as usual. But for some reason this time I became emotional. I continued listening intently and singing along. I was feeling God's presence in a powerful way through the music.

God is always present, but I'm not always aware of it. Is it because I am not open to the divine presence? Am I too distracted by other thoughts or concerns in my life?

Regardless of what we feel, whether at worship, home, work or school, God is with us. We know that's true because today's quoted verse tells us so, and Hebrews 13:5 declares, '[God] will never leave you or abandon you.'

We need to keep our hearts and minds open to God's presence; otherwise we may miss seeing God at work in everyday moments. How many times have I missed God's presence because I was mentally or physically distracted? While I don't always feel God's presence like I did in church that day, I am now more conscious of staying open and focused on the working of God minute by minute, day by day.

Prayer: *Dear God, we are thankful for your constant presence in our lives. May we continue to honour you and seek you as we live each day in faithful obedience. Amen*

Thought for the day: Today I will focus my attention on what God is doing in my life.

Brian Foster (North Carolina, USA)

Is this mine?

Read Matthew 7:7–11

He who did not spare his own Son, but gave him up for us all – how will he not also, along with him, graciously give us all things?
Romans 8:32 (NIV)

'Is this mine?' piped a little voice behind the wobbly sandcastles on the beach. My three-year-old great-niece was enjoying playing with the new blue sand-scooping hippo toy I had bought. She preferred this to the dumper truck and other gifts which her cousin had monopolised. Reassured, she continued her play, content in the knowledge that she would take home her newly acquired treasure. It would belong to her. It would always be hers to enjoy.

Her question replayed in my mind throughout the day. I found myself wondering whether I regard God's good gifts in the same way. Are they really mine? Have I learnt to accept them each day? Can I own them, use them and enjoy them?

The Bible underpins the promised gifts of God with reminders of his character of pure goodness and love. God graciously gives and gives. He is unable to do otherwise. We can know God's complete forgiveness. He gives the Holy Spirit's loving presence to live within us. He is constantly at work in our lives, lavishing his gifts of grace for ministry and service.

Is all this as truly mine, as it could be? Am I enjoying all that God has given?

Prayer: *Father God, you have given us all we need in Jesus. Guide us in using your good gifts to serve you.*

Thought for the day: The Father knows the things that I need.

Hilary Allen (England, United Kingdom)

Tiny seeds

Read Luke 13:18–21

'[The kingdom of God] is like a mustard seed that someone took and sowed in the garden; it grew and became a tree, and the birds of the air made nests in its branches.'
Luke 13:19 (NRSV)

After finishing a sandwich one day, I saw a poppy seed from the crust roll across the palm of my hand. It was so tiny, and I marvelled at the idea that it contained everything necessary to grow a flower. This made me think of Jesus' words about how faith as small as a mustard seed can grow into something much larger and more fruitful.

Growth in the kingdom of God is often a slow process. Just as we may not notice a seed turning into a tree or flower, we tend not to notice miracles as they develop. God's miracles surround us, but they usually take time. We may offer someone a kind word, a listening ear or a testimony of our faith, only to find years later that the seed was held dear and grew into something that helped them enormously.

Amazingly, if we scatter the seeds, God can produce great things. Let us consider our responses to others carefully because if we speak and act with gentleness and faith, we might be astonished at what wonders can grow from those tiny seeds.

Prayer: *Dear God, help us always to be willing to give you the little faith we have so that you can use it for good. Amen*

Thought for the day: God can grow something wonderful from my tiny seeds of faith.

Keren Dibbens-Wyatt (England, United Kingdom)

Forgiveness

Read Colossians 3:12–14

Confess your sins to one another, and pray for one another, so that you may be healed.
James 5:16 (NRSV)

'You are forgiven.' When I heard those words, a burden of guilt was lifted from me. I had called a longtime friend to confess a wrong that I had committed against him 51 years before.

I had confessed the sin to God, but I had never admitted it to my friend until now. I had waited all these years to tell him because I was embarrassed and ashamed of what I had done. Knowing that he was a faithful Christian, I felt confident that he would respond the way he did. If I had just admitted my sin to him when it occurred, I might not have had to carry that guilt for so many years.

The Bible tells us to confess our sins to God *and* to one another. It is much easier to confess to God than to a person. After all, God promises to forgive us. This is a certainty that we don't have when it comes to other people. But I believe the Bible tells us to confess to our brothers and sisters so that both parties can heal. I am truly thankful for God's forgiveness and for forgiveness from people I have wronged.

Prayer: *Merciful God, thank you for forgiving us when we sincerely confess to you. Thank you also for the forgiveness of others. Help us all to move towards the wholeness that you offer. Amen*

Thought for the day: Whom do I need to ask for forgiveness today?

Bob Alderson (Oklahoma, USA)

PRAYER FOCUS: THOSE BURDENED BY GUILT

Soaring

Read Isaiah 40:27–31

Those who hope in the Lord will renew their strength. They will soar on wings like eagles; they will run and not grow weary, they will walk and not be faint.

Isaiah 40:31 (NIV)

While walking one morning, I noticed a hawk flying low with a little bird flitting around it. I was immediately concerned for the small bird because I was unsure how the hawk would react. As I continued watching, I witnessed an unforgettable sight. The hawk swooped down, and the little bird landed on the hawk's back. The hawk and its passenger then soared across the road in front of me. After a short while, the hawk swooped down once more by a barbed wire fence, where the little bird dismounted and landed on the top strand. The hawk continued on, soaring higher than ever, and soon was out of sight. After a brief rest, the little bird began its flight again and was soon soaring.

I immediately praised God for allowing me to see this beautiful illustration of one of my favourite verses. We all grow weary. But when we feel that we can't go on, scripture encourages us to put our hope in God. God is aware of and concerned for our plight. Just as the little bird appeared to gather strength from resting on the hawk and was able to continue his journey, we can trust God to renew our strength, enabling us to continue. Then, with our hope and strength renewed, we too can begin to soar.

Prayer: *Thank you, Lord, for renewing our strength when we place our hope in you. Amen*

Thought for the day: Where do I find strength for my journey?

Marsha Howard (Texas, USA)

Relax

Read Mark 4:35–41

[Jesus] got up, rebuked the wind and said to the waves, 'Quiet! Be still!' Then the wind died down and it was completely calm.
Mark 4:39 (NIV)

I recently watched my little boy as he tried unsuccessfully to get the wheel of his homemade toy to work. He got so frustrated that he gave up, tossed it aside and burst into tears.

His outburst reminded me of my own frustrating battles. Things didn't seem to be working for me either. From relationship challenges to issues related to being between jobs, my plate was full. I was tempted to toss everything aside like my son did and give up in frustration.

Yet through all the noise in my head and the storms around me, one word remained distinct: *relax*. A still, small voice kept whispering to me, 'Relax.' But being a restless person, I desperately wanted to do something to fix the situation. I tried various approaches, all to no avail.

So I finally decided to turn to the One who calmed the storm. I decided to obey his word and listen to his wise counsel. I know that with Christ in my ship, I can safely reach the other shore. I have not arrived yet. Although the storms still rage, I know with Christ I need not fret.

Prayer: *Christ Jesus, be with us in our storms. Help us to trust in your will and your ways. Amen*

Thought for the day: Even when storms rage, I will cast my cares on Christ and relax.

Chiazo Obiudu (Ebonyi State, Nigeria)

God's answer

Read Philippians 4:4–9

The peace of God, which surpasses all understanding, will guard your hearts and your minds in Christ Jesus.
Philippians 4:7 (NRSV)

My family was celebrating the birth of our second child, a healthy baby boy. Then, in less than two weeks, we were fearful we were losing him after such a short time. At just 13 days old he contracted respiratory syncytial virus (RSV). My son was fighting for his life, and I was powerless to help him.

The first night that he was in pediatric intensive care we were not allowed to touch or hold him. I can clearly recall the turmoil I felt inside. I also clearly recall the soothing peace that I felt as our pastor and prayer group called. We took the moment to pray together, and that moment of prayer helped to ease my fear. We prayed that the peace and understanding the apostle Paul spoke of would guard our hearts. While the remainder of the time my son spent in the hospital before coming home would be difficult, our prayer on the first night helped ease our fears.

In moments of anxiety and fear it is easy to lose sight of God's presence. But when we feel that life is spiralling out of control, we will find peace when we bring our struggle to God in prayer.

Prayer: *Dear Lord, today we are afraid. But we know that in all things you are with us. Fill our hearts with your peace. Thank you for the care you have given us through the gift of Jesus Christ. In his name we pray. Amen*

Thought for the day: Prayer is our God-given answer to fear.

Jeffrey Krodel (Pennsylvania, USA)

Jesus, prince of peace

Read 1 Kings 1:32–40

Those who went ahead and those who followed shouted, 'Hosanna!'
'Blessed is he who comes in the name of the Lord!' 'Blessed is the
coming kingdom of our father David!' 'Hosanna in the highest heaven!'
Mark 11:9–10 (NIV)

I learned as a child that Jesus' humble entry into Jerusalem on a donkey fulfilled Zechariah's prophecy (see Zechariah 9:9). As a young adult, I discovered that he was also following in the footsteps of King David's son Solomon. The crowd hailed Jesus as the son of David and the hoped-for messiah. Many of them wanted him to overthrow the oppressive Roman government, but they were to be disappointed. Jesus taught love for God and neighbour. His followers discovered that Christ was the prince of peace and, more than a military leader, he was 'the way and the truth and the life' (John 14:6).

Jesus preached good news to the poor and to all nations. After his death and resurrection, his disciples took that good news to all parts of the Roman empire and then around the world. Christ's message of God's universal sovereignty and love for all people has persisted despite the violence in the world and sometimes even within the church. We live in an era of fear and nationalism, but God is calling us to something greater. When we love people from all backgrounds, we truly honour Christ as the prince of peace and Messiah.

Prayer: *Dear Jesus, thank you for coming into the world to proclaim God's love for all people and nations. Help us to embody your love. Amen*

Thought for the day: I will honour the prince of peace by loving someone who is unlike me today.

Sister Confianza del Señor (Colón, Honduras)

Hearing God's voice

Read John 10:1–6

O that today you would listen to [God's] voice!
Psalm 95:7 (NRSV)

On my first trip to India, my wife, Linda, would call each morning. It was the longest time we had ever been apart, and speaking with her helped me to make it through each day. I felt weighed down when we failed to connect and counted the hours until her call the next day.

When we spoke, however, just the sound of her voice would energise me. During my travels, I replayed each word of our morning conversation. Preaching in sweltering heat, I meditated on the stories Linda had shared. Drifting off to sleep at night, I anticipated her next call. Linda's voice carried me through the lonely moments of our three weeks apart.

Likewise, the voice of Jesus brings strength during our darkest days. Psalm 95:7 challenges us to 'listen to God's voice!' Jesus declares that 'my sheep hear my voice' (John 10:27). Just as hearing Linda's voice made a huge difference in my day, a word from Jesus encourages us.

On those days when we feel lonely or discouraged, we can take an extra moment to listen for the Lord's voice. The lines of communication are always open, and God's voice has the power to transform us.

Prayer: *Dear Lord, open our ears to hear your voice in the midst of our noisy, chaotic world. Amen*

Thought for the day: Today I will take extra time to listen for God's voice.

Barney Cargile III (California, USA)

Who am I?

Read Exodus 3:7–14

Moses said to God, 'Who am I that I should go to Pharaoh and bring the Israelites out of Egypt?' And God said, 'I will be with you.'
Exodus 3:11–12 (NIV)

I have missed opportunities to share my faith. I turned down an invitation to lead a Bible study. I chose to stay silent when someone was in need of comfort. My reticence came from a deep feeling of being unworthy. Surely God would want a different messenger.

Moses experienced similar reluctance. When God asked him to lead Israel out of slavery, Moses responded with doubt and excuses: 'Who am I? I would say the wrong things. What if nobody listens?' God responded by turning the focus away from Moses. God assured Moses, 'I will be with you' and taught him the words he should say. When Moses worried that he would be ignored, 'God said to Moses, "I am who I am."'

Many of us can relate to Moses and his feelings of fear and inadequacy. Maybe we think we should wait until we feel capable to serve God. This story reminds me of the truth: by ourselves we are never going to be good enough. But God still chooses us. And, in God, we are more than enough. When Moses tried to act on his own, his people rejected him and he was banished from Egypt. But when he returned at God's command, a nation followed him. With God's help, we can do whatever God has planned for us.

Prayer: *Dear Father, we confess our reluctance to follow you and share our faith. Help us to remember that you are with us. Amen*

Thought for the day: With God to help me, I am more than enough.

Cindy Tanquary Peavy (Alabama, USA)

Thinking on target

Read Isaiah 26:3–8

You will keep in perfect peace those whose minds are steadfast, because they trust in you.
Isaiah 26:3 (NIV)

I pushed myself to ride rugged single-track bike trails far beyond what I'd ever done. Switchback turns, jagged rocks, tight spaces between trees, quick inclines and descents just kept coming. I barely navigated one obstacle before another was right in front of me. What had I gotten myself into?

Thankfully I had a kind and experienced guide riding ahead of me. He let me know what was coming and gave tips on how to navigate each obstacle. At one point, he told me about target fixation, a term I'd never heard.

He explained that our bodies gravitate towards our point of focus. If I kept my eyes fixed on the rock in the trail, I'd likely hit it straight on and launch off the bike. But if I concentrated farther down the way, aware of the rock yet not staring right at it, I could safely veer around it. After a while, I began to understand. Rather than nervously approaching a narrow passage between tree trunks, I forced myself to look ahead. I cleared it with no problem and cheered out loud!

Scripture speaks of keeping our focus on God and not on our troubles, which is easier said than done. But the Lord promises peace as we fill our minds with truth rather than our worries. Life's struggles are still there, but God gives hope and strength to see us through.

Prayer: *Dear Lord, help us to remember and cling to your promises. Fill our minds with your truth so that we may experience your peace. Amen*

Thought for the day: Today, I will focus my thoughts on God's word instead of my worries.

Lee Ann Zanon (Oregon, USA)

God's ways and ours

Read Isaiah 55:1–9

'As the heavens are higher than the earth, so are my ways higher than your ways and my thoughts than your thoughts.'
Isaiah 55:9 (NRSV)

My six-year-old likes to watch Disney Channel movies. However, since English is not our first language, she often asks me questions about the plot or characters. Despite my best efforts, she often finds my explanations confusing because of her limited understanding of the world.

Just as my daughter struggles to comprehend my explanations of her favourite movies, we sometimes find it difficult to understand God's action and presence in our lives. When we experience hardship or do not see the answer to our prayers, we wonder why God has not responded. This is because God's ways and our ways are so different. The nature of divinity is impossible for us to fully understand.

We must remember that it is not our responsibility to try to figure out the reason behind God's actions. We may ask, 'Why do you let this happen to me?' But as children of God, we are simply asked to have faith: to fully believe in our divine parent who loves us. We can do this because God's decisions are always meant for our good.

Prayer: *Dear God, help us to believe in your plans even when we do not understand them. Amen*

Thought for the day: When faced with questions, I will trust in God.

Denny Pranolo (West Java, Indonesia)

Never alone

Read Romans 8:14–17

I am convinced that neither death nor life, neither angels nor demons, neither the present nor the future, nor any powers, neither height nor depth, nor anything else in all creation, will be able to separate us from the love of God that is in Christ Jesus our Lord.
Romans 8:38–39 (NIV)

As I write these words, the world is facing the Covid-19 pandemic. Millions of people around the world are in quarantine, and many thousands have died. Fearful and confused people can be seen racing for cleaning supplies and necessities at the store. But we need to remember in our suffering and times of fear that nothing can separate us from God's love. No matter what trial we face, God's love and care for us will outshine any darkness.

God does not promise that we will not face hardships. In fact, the Bible even notes how we will suffer as God's children. Yet the book of Romans tells of our inheritance of God's kingdom and how, though troubles will come, we are promised to share in Christ's glory.

Today when we face darkness we may feel fearful, worried or anxious. But each time these emotions arise, we can remind ourselves whose we are. We are the beloved children of the creator of the world. We can cry out, 'Abba, Father,' and God listens to our concerns. God is stronger than anything we are facing today.

Prayer: *Thank you, God, that we can give our burdens to you. You have power over every fear we have. When all we can see is darkness, we praise you for your never-failing light. Amen*

Thought for the day: Nothing can separate us from God's love.

Alyssa Fritschy (Florida, USA)

PRAYER FOCUS: FAMILIES WHO HAVE LOST LOVED ONES TO COVID-19

Leave that with me

Read Genesis 39:1–6
Leave all your worries with him, because he cares for you.
1 Peter 5:7 (GNT)

Since my husband died, my son has helpfully handled many of my affairs. Before each of his visits, I make a note of my concerns and then, as we talk, I tell him each one. 'Leave that with me,' he'll say, so I do just that. Eventually, I have crossed every item off my list.

By the time my son's visit is over, I'm at peace. Later on, it doesn't occur to me to check up and see if he's handling my requests. I know and trust him, and he has not let me down.

High-ranking Potiphar had a similar trust in Joseph, his personal servant. So strong was his confidence that 'he did not concern himself with anything except the food he ate' (Genesis 39:6). Potiphar's trust is a tribute to diligent Joseph, who never let him down.

As I come to God, bringing my requests, may I give him the tribute of my trust. May I not check up later to see if he is working on my behalf, but rather rest in the certainty of a wise outcome.

Prayer: *Lord, may we leave our worries with you, and then rest in the knowledge that you do all things well. Amen*

Thought for the day: God carefully notes my requests, and is skilled at handling them in the very best way.

Elaine Brown (Scotland, United Kingdom)

Significance of the cross

Read Romans 5:6–11

There is now no condemnation for those who are in Christ Jesus, because through Christ Jesus the law of the Spirit who gives life has set you free from the law of sin and death.
Romans 8:1–2 (NIV)

I began attending seminary after I retired, taking one autumn-semester class. I have done that annually for the last eight years. My purpose is not to attain a degree; it's simply to help me grow in my walk with the Lord.

As friends heard about my seminary experience, they often asked, 'What have you learned?' After much reflection, I named some aspects of my faith that have grown in importance to me. The first is reading and properly interpreting the Bible. The second is humility, learning from the powerful example of Jesus. Being in community, living and serving together as the body of Christ is another. And finally, the significance of the cross has become clearer to me. For Christians, what Christ did at Calvary assures us of eternal life. We don't earn it; it's a gift by the grace of God. But the cross is about more than our personal salvation. It's the point in history where God intervened to renew the covenant with creation, the day that sin and death were conquered.

I've read about the cross of Christ and what it means; I believe it, and I confess it. But the more I reflect on that sacrifice, the more sure I am that I will never fully comprehend this act of incredible love and amazing grace.

Prayer: *Heavenly Father, thank you for the gift of your Son, Jesus Christ. Help us to share the good news of the gospel with others. Amen*

Thought for the day: What am I doing to grow in my faith today?

John D. Bown (Minnesota, USA)

Be not dismayed

Read Psalm 121

Fear thou not; for I am with thee: be not dismayed; for I am thy God: I will strengthen thee; yea, I will help thee; I will uphold thee with the right hand of my righteousness.
Isaiah 41:10 (KJV)

I woke up on a January morning in 1996 to find my husband of 32 years having a seizure. That morning my world collapsed.

After being in intensive care for two months, he was sent to a rehab centre where I was trained to be his caregiver in our home. It took two weeks of full-time care for me to realise that this plan was not sustainable. I remember sitting on my sofa exhausted and feeling like a bird in a cage.

I began calling a list of caregivers, but it seemed everyone was either unavailable or too expensive. Finally, a young woman said she could help me and would charge an amount I could afford. She came over that day and allowed me to rest.

I did not get the miracle of healing for my husband that I prayed for each day, but God was with me through it all. My husband died roughly a year later. While my life changed forever that one January morning, God has led me through more than 20 years of being a widow. However, I know that I am never alone with God by my side.

Prayer: *O Emmanuel, thank you for hearing our prayers and walking alongside us. Amen*

Thought for the day: Even when my world collapses, God is with me.

B. Beauchamp (Texas, USA)

Towards the light

Read Luke 8:16–18

When Jesus spoke again to the people, he said, 'I am the light of the world. Whoever follows me will never walk in darkness, but will have the light of life.'
John 8:12 (NIV)

Every evening at bedtime I head towards my room and switch off the lights along the way. Years ago I lost my sight in one eye, and my remaining vision is dimming with age. But despite the dark, I am confident that I will not trip or fall as I head towards the light shining from my destination because it illuminates my way. If I remember something that I have forgotten and turn back, I am immediately in trouble because my body blocks the light and I am walking in my own shadow.

This reminds me of my daily walk with Jesus. For over 64 years, since I was a teenager, I have tried to walk towards God's light. But when I have turned away and walked in the shadow of my own choices and actions, I have often been in trouble. It is awesome to know that no matter how dark it is, we are always able to find God's light by turning towards our Lord in our actions and prayers.

Prayer: *Lord of light, guide us so that we may walk in the brilliance of your presence. We pray as Jesus taught us, 'Our Father in heaven, hallowed be your name, your kingdom come, your will be done on earth as it is in heaven. Give us today our daily bread. Forgive us our debts, as we also have forgiven our debtors. And lead us not into temptation, but deliver us from the evil one.'* Amen*

Thought for the day: The light of Jesus' love guides me on my way.

Keith Honeyman (Western Cape, South Africa)

PRAYER FOCUS: THOSE WHO HAVE TROUBLE SEEING
*Matthew 6:9–13

Careful witness

Read Colossians 4:2–6

Let your conversation be always full of grace, seasoned with salt, so that you may know how to answer everyone.
Colossians 4:6 (NIV)

I have three very good friends. We have known each other for over 30 years and have been through many things together: births of children; deaths of family members; job changes; multiple moves; many long, serious conversations; and many deep, hearty laughs. The four of us are as close as sisters, but there is one challenge – two of us are Christians and two of us are not.

My Christian friend and I often strive to witness with our words and actions when we are all together, and we have prayed for opportunities to share our faith with our dear friends. We have tried to 'make the most of every opportunity' to talk about God's work in our lives – how God gives us strength and wisdom and walks beside us. We have also prayed we would 'be wise in the way we act' towards our friends. The importance of being God's ambassadors is not lost on us. We know that our actions likely speak louder than our words in our witness.

Although it sometimes pains us to see our efforts not bear fruit, we have faith and peace knowing God's work is not complete and the answer is in God's hands. We are committed to doing God's work by letting our conversation be always full of grace and seasoned with salt.

Prayer: *Dear God, help us to witness by our words and actions. May you make us into ambassadors for you. Amen*

Thought for the day: I will continue to look for ways to share the good news.

Jennifer Lanane (North Carolina, USA)

Trust in the Lord

Read Jeremiah 29:11–14

'I know the plans I have for you,' declares the Lord, 'plans to prosper you and not to harm you, plans to give you hope and a future.'
Jeremiah 29:11 (NIV)

We will send our beloved dog Marley to my parents' house soon. My husband was given a new international assignment by his employer so we will be moving and cannot take her with us. It is hard sending Marley away, but we are comforted to know that she will be loved by my parents and all the other family members who live near them. While Marley doesn't have any knowledge of her future, we are preparing everything in her best interests.

I realised that, just like Marley, I am loved and my parent in heaven is preparing everything for me. While it is still hard for me to leave the comfortable life we have in our own country, I can step into uncertainty knowing that God is with me. We may not always understand why things happen the way they do. Sometimes, all we can do is trust and obey.

Through caring for my beloved dog, the Lord has shown me a piece of God's heart. God is so good! We cannot fully grasp God's love for us, but our creator wants us to understand that we are loved and that God cares about our future.

Prayer: *Dear Lord, when we cannot understand the things that are happening, give us strength to trust and obey you. Amen*

Thought for the day: God cares about my future and will prepare the way.

Lei Cao Garcia-Bote (Kuala Lumpur, Malaysia)

Planting seeds

Read Mark 4:1–9

[Jesus] also said, 'The kingdom of God is as if someone would scatter seed on the ground, and would sleep and rise night and day, and the seed would sprout and grow.'
Mark 4:26–27 (NRSV)

In my retirement I have found that planting flower and vegetable seeds is a good way of relating to God and creation. Planting can be a time of meditation as I prepare the soil and plant or scatter the seeds. Then comes the patient waiting and hoping for the germination and sprouting of the seeds, followed by the joy of seeing the seeds turn into plants, with buds, blooms and fruit.

Growing relationships is a lot like gardening. We sow seeds of kindness through seeing every person as one created in the image of God and thus kin to us. We sow words of kindness by speaking the truth in love. We do deeds of kindness by actively treating every person with compassion and respect – as we would like to be treated. Thinking about all this led me to Jesus' parable of the sower. In the parable, the sower scattered the seed everywhere, regardless of the condition of the soil. We can do likewise. Then, as with gardening, we watch, wait and hope for joyful growth in our relationships with others and with God.

Prayer: *Help us, God, to be generous in our thoughts, words and deeds to everyone we meet today. Then may your love bring a harvest of loving and reconciled relationships. Amen*

Thought for the day: Today I will sow seeds of kindness then wait and hope for joyful growth.

John Sawyer (South Carolina, USA)

My rainbow Bible

Read Psalm 119:105–112

Your word is a lamp for my feet, a light on my path.
Psalm 119:105 (NIV)

About ten years ago I casually picked up a copy of *The Upper Room* at my church. I enjoyed the daily meditations written by people around the world who shared honestly about faith, forgiveness, challenge and many other facets of their relationship with God. In an old Bible, I began to mark each daily scripture reading with a different colour so that I could locate it again easily.

A decade into this process, I am still doing the daily readings, transforming my old Bible into a rainbow of yellow, pink, orange and blue. To my surprise, there are few chapters that are not filled with evidence of the verses I've read, and I can find relevant passages quickly and easily. I am amazed at how much I've read without even trying!

Best of all, reading these devotionals and colour-coding my Bible have helped my faith. The daily testimonials about Christ's workings encourage me to think about how he might be moving in my life. They also encourage me to faithfully pursue Christ's call to help the poor, welcome the stranger, feed the hungry, love my neighbour and worship with others. I am learning that God is alive and at work – in other people's lives and in my own.

Prayer: *Dear Lord, help us to learn from the writers who share their faith in these pages. Reveal to us how you are active in our lives. Amen*

Thought for the day: Daily spiritual practices yield abundant results.

Abigail Gary (Pennsylvania, USA)

Longed for

Read Matthew 18:10–14

In the same way your Father in heaven is not willing that any of these little ones should perish.
Matthew 18:14 (NIV)

I lead activities sessions for adults with learning disabilities. One day, a woman in my care walked off the site without my noticing. She was nowhere to be found, and I was frantic. We searched the streets around the site and those leading into the city, and we called the police. All the while, my worst fears for her were racing through my mind, 'What if… ?' Then the news came over the police radio that she'd been found. What a relief! I later learned that she had made her way to a tea shop near the centre of town, where she had been kindly looked after by staff and a caring customer.

The range of emotions I felt that day – from fear and dread to sheer joy and relief at the news of her safety – must have been close to those experienced by the shepherd in Jesus' story. The Father knows how easily we can wander, and what snares and dangers await us when we do. But God knows and cares for us individually, having deep regard for the choices we make and the difficulties we face. Matthew 18 reminds us that we are known and wanted by our loving God, who rejoices when we are found.

Prayer: *Loving God, thank you for caring for those who are lost and wandering. Help us to love them as you do. Amen*

Thought for the day: God will help me through any difficulty I face.

Rupert Greville (England, United Kingdom)

Working to honour God

Read Colossians 3:18–25
Whatever you do, work at it with all your heart, as working for the Lord, not for human masters.
Colossians 3:23 (NIV)

When I was 13, I went to live with my aunt and uncle on their farm. One of my daily tasks was to strap a long burlap sack across my body and pick corn until the sack was full and heavy. Then while Aunt Elsie made supper, I sat on a stool in the kitchen, shucking and dividing the corn – some for the pigs, some for us and some to give away. After sorting, I hauled the pigs' corn out and threw it over the fence to them. I would much rather have been with my friends – swimming, going to the movies, having fun.

Every evening before bedtime, Aunt Elsie read the Bible out loud. One evening as she read Colossians 3, the words in today's quoted verse sank in. I went to bed ashamed for resenting the farm work. My relatives were generous and loving. They took me in without knowing me well. They didn't order me to do chores; they asked. They honoured the Lord with their work. I had begun helping them out of boredom but ended up helping out of love. Instead of resenting the chores, I grew to love both the work and the animals.

I will never forget the peace and joy I experienced on that farm. My aunt and uncle left me with a gentle reminder that we honour God by dedicating whatever work we do to the Lord.

Prayer: *Dear Father, thank you for giving us work and a purpose. Help us to do whatever you set before us with the peace and joy that only honouring you can bring. Amen*

Thought for the day: Today I will honour God in whatever I do.

Jo Davis (Missouri, USA)

Trust the harness!

Read Matthew 11:25–30

'Come to me, all you who are struggling hard and carrying heavy loads, and I will give you rest.'
Matthew 11:28 (CEB)

Many years ago I took a rock climbing course at a local college. The instructor put me in a harness and instructed me to climb to the top of the wall. He told me upon reaching the top to then lean back in the harness and rappel back down the wall. The instructor emphasised that I must trust the harness to prevent my falling. He warned me not to hold on to the wall but to lean back and surrender all of my weight to the harness. But instead of trusting the harness, I knocked up against the wall with my left shoulder. By transferring my weight from the harness to my shoulder, I injured myself.

   I believe this same concept holds true in our lives as Christians. Christ wishes for us to trust him, completely surrendering our lives to him. By doing so we will find the peace that can come to us only from turning our lives over to his will. My lack of trust in my harness caused physical injury; but our failure to trust our lives completely to Christ will result in spiritual injury, depriving us of the peace and rest Christ offers.

Prayer: *Dear Jesus, today we pray for the strength and the will to trust you and to surrender our lives to you. Amen*

Thought for the day: Jesus is the only way to true peace.

Tony Lotito (Virginia, USA)

Rebuilding God's house

Read Haggai 1:3–11

My house lies in ruins, while all of you hurry off to your own houses.
Haggai 1:9 (NRSV)

My church has recently undergone a split where about half of the congregation has left for a variety of reasons ranging from doctrinal disagreements to personality differences.

In today's reading Haggai challenged the governor and the high priest about their priorities. The temple that had been demolished by the Babylonians when Judah went into exile had lain in ruins ever since. Then Haggai intervened.

These verses challenged me regarding the situation of my church. Amid the rubble of hurt, questions and doubt there is also a sense of growth and rebuilding. So I asked myself, 'How can I be involved in rebuilding our congregation?' I can participate in the many prayer sessions, Bible studies and activities. I can invite friends to come with me and share Christ with others more often. I can offer a positive outlook when negativity emerges, and I can support our pastors.

When we are willing to participate in rebuilding rather than simply attending to our own desires, we can rebuild our church – renewing our faith in the process.

Prayer: *Dear Father, help us to focus on you today and what you would have us do to bring renewed life to your beloved community on earth. Amen*

Thought for the day: How will I participate in building God's beloved community today?

Dianne Fegan (Queensland, Australia)

In all circumstances

Read Psalm 29

Rejoice always, pray without ceasing, give thanks in all circumstances; for this is the will of God in Christ Jesus for you.
1 Thessalonians 5:16–18 (NRSV)

Spending the night with my 92-year-old dad in his hospital room was a hectic experience. Between temperature checks, blood pressure checks, the noise of the ventilator tubes, medication alarms and nurses taking blood samples, I realised I would not get much sleep.

Dad was diagnosed with congestive heart failure and fluid was building up around his lungs, making it hard for him to breathe. As I watched him lying in bed labouring to breathe in the early morning hours, I realised that I had forgotten my nightly prayers. I began to pray for Dad's recovery. I praised God for Dad's 92 years of life and for all the years I have had with him. Immediately I felt a sense of calm amid all the noise and activity.

Sometimes we get so caught up in the frenetic activity of life that we forget to pray and praise God for what God has done in us and through us. When we find ourselves overwhelmed by the frenzy, we do well to recall Paul's words: 'Pray without ceasing, give thanks in [not *for*] all circumstances.'

Prayer: *Almighty and merciful God, help us always to make time for you, no matter how noisy and hectic our days become. Thank you for the peace you give us when we spend time with you. Amen*

Thought for the day: I won't let the confusion of life keep me from communion with God.

Henry L. Childress (Arkansas, USA)

Such grace!

Read John 13:1–6

After that, he poured water into a basin and began to wash his disciples' feet, drying them with the towel that was wrapped round him.

John 13:5 (NIV)

I live near the beach, and my husband and I regularly go for walks along the shore. Once, my husband forgot to change from his open-toed sandals and when we arrived at the shore the tide was coming in fast. We had to walk on the shingle. Every few steps he stopped to shake the tiny stones from between his toes or under his foot. There were many cries of 'Ouch' and 'Ooh!'

When we reached the road, he took off his sandals to wipe his feet. The tiny, sharp stones had stuck to every part of his feet along with the damp sand. We had no towel, only an old paper tissue in my pocket, which I gladly handed over and sat laughing as he rubbed as much off as he could.

When I read the verses in today's passage, I see that Jesus did not stand by laughing when the disciples arrived with dusty, dirty feet. He did not hand over a towel or call a servant to do the dirty work. He gently took their feet himself and washed and dried them. And he even washed and dried the feet of Judas, the man who would betray him a few hours later. The king of kings and lord of lords, and yet our humble servant.

Such grace!

Prayer: *Dear God, give us your Spirit of humility and grace, that we may love as Jesus did. Amen*

Thought for the day: Now that the Lord has washed my feet, I should wash other's feet.

Pam Lewis (England, United Kingdom)

Expectations

Read Psalm 143:1–10

Let the morning bring me word of your unfailing love, for I have put my trust in you. Show me the way I should go, for to you I entrust my life.

Psalm 143:8 (NIV)

Usually when I say, 'I trust you,' what I mean is: 'I'm counting on you to do what I want or expect,' or, 'I trust you to get this job done on time,' or, 'I trust you will pay back what you owe.' Naturally, I do the same thing when I talk to God: 'I trust you not to let my plane crash,' or, 'I trust you will heal my friend.'

A while back, someone I loved had a problem. I prayed and tried to trust God to fix it. It seemed like the right thing to do, but I got a shock one night when that quiet voice in my head said, 'Trusting God doesn't mean laying out your expectations and believing God will do what you want. It means laying *down* your expectations and trusting God.' This was a scary yet strangely freeing thought. After all, God knows the future and loves us. Psalm 143:8 doesn't say, 'Give me what I want because I trust you.' It says, 'Show me the way I should go, for to you I entrust my life.' David was asking God to show him the way and help him to follow. He even entrusted his life to God. If David could truly trust, surely I can too!

Prayer: *Heavenly Father, teach us to lay down our expectations and trust you to do what is best for us. Amen*

Thought for the day: I trust God when I lay down my expectations and follow God's ways.

Heather Tekavec (British Columbia, Canada)

Small group questions

Wednesday 5 January

1 How do you begin your prayers? Do you pray differently when you have a particular need? Why or why not?

2 When do you expect an immediate answer to your prayers? How do you avoid transactional prayer? What helps you to accept God's timing and appreciate the blessings you have right now?

3 Is it easier for you to thank God for what you have or to ask God for things? Why? What helps you remain grateful and content with what God has already given you?

4 When you or a loved one has an urgent need, how do you stay mindful of God's goodness and generosity? When answers do not come as you hoped or within the time frame that you hoped, what spiritual practices help you to remain at peace?

5 What would happen if you began expressing gratitude first and asking for something last in situations or relationships in your life? In what ways could it make a positive difference?

Wednesday 12 January

1 What labels have you been given? Do you find yourself living into the labels others give you, or do labels not affect you much? Why?

2 Who sees the potential in you? How does their perspective of you change the way you view yourself? How does it change the way others view you?

3 Describe a time you have experienced or witnessed a transformation from God. What positive changes occurred? How do you know the transformation came from God?

4 What does it mean to you that you are called and redeemed by God? How does knowing you are a child of God change the way you think about yourself?

5 How can you be more intentional about seeing good in others? In what ways can you encourage others to embrace their identity in Christ and to see their potential?

Wednesday 19 January

1 When you find yourself frustrated with others, what helps you remember to look at them with patience and love? How do you avoid dwelling on your frustration?

2 Do you ever find yourself becoming irritated when people do things differently from the way you would do them? What scriptures and prayers help you to manage your irritation in such situations?

3 How does your outlook change when you focus on God's love for us all? Who or what helps you to remain focused on God's love and forgiveness? In what ways do you actively seek to extend God's love and forgiveness to others?

4 What does it mean to you to have a generous heart towards others? Who in scripture best exemplifies having a generous heart?

5 Why is it sometimes easier to focus on the speck in another person's eye instead of the plank in our own? When have you seen a wonderful example of love and forgiveness? What makes it so memorable?

Wednesday 26 January

1 What scripture passages encourage you when you are living through painful situations? What comfort do these passages give you?

2 Name a time when you prayed fervently for healing but did not receive the answer you wanted. Why do you think you received a different answer? Describe what effect, if any, this had on your relationship with God.

3 How have you found yourself changed and comforted by prayer? In what ways does it encourage you to think about prayer as not

just about the future but as something that can change you in the present?

4　What scripture passages do you wrestle with? Why? How does your understanding of the passages change the more you dwell on them? How is it beneficial to study scripture this way?

5　How does reminding yourself of God's past faithfulness help you to accept your current experiences? What spiritual practices encourage you to place your confidence in God's love?

Wednesday 2 February

1　Are you musically inclined? Do you enjoy singing as a form of worship, or do you prefer other forms of worship? Why?

2　What part of worship tends to feel like a traditional formality? What can you do at your next worship service to enjoy that part of worship more fully?

3　Who in scripture worshipped God with joy and thanksgiving? What scripture verses best remind you of the importance of joyful worship?

4　Describe a time when you heard God's voice or felt God open your heart during worship. What was the experience like? How did it change the way you worship?

5　Who in your life has encouraged you to worship in new and different ways? How have you been blessed by these new ways of worshipping God?

Wednesday 9 February

1　When have you helped someone who did not have anyone else to help them? Why did you choose to offer help? How did they respond?

2 Do you find it easy or difficult to serve others? Why? What prayers help you to humbly serve those around you?

3 Who in your community needs help today? How can you serve them? How can you show them God's love and care?

4 When has someone's act of service towards you changed the way you serve others? What is the most powerful act of service that you have witnessed or received?

5 What service opportunities does your church offer? Are you active in these ministries? How does your church help you find opportunities to show God's love to others?

Wednesday 16 February

1 Do social media and other forms of technology make you feel more connected to others or more isolated from them? When have you experienced loneliness in recent years? What possible connections do you see between social media and loneliness?

2 When you experience loneliness, what helps you to deal with it?

3 Do you feel that God's law of love illuminates your shortcomings? If so, in what ways? How do you strive to live out this law of love each day?

4 How easy is it for you to become captivated by virtual connections? Why do you think those kinds of connections are so appealing to us? How do you actively seek to give more time and attention to those who are near to you physically?

5 How does it encourage you to know that when you work together with the broader Christian community, your individual efforts go further? When have you seen Christians come together to make a more significant difference as a group than they would have individually?

Wednesday 23 February

1 When have you judged someone negatively based on their appearance? What did you do when you realised you had judged them negatively?

2 How does focusing on the humanity and depth of a person help you to love them? When have you changed your opinion about someone by thinking of them in this way?

3 Are you encouraged to know that Christ died for you and loves you no matter who you are? How does that knowledge change the way you think and act?

4 How do you strive to emulate Jesus' example of loving everyone we meet? Name specific ways you will show love to others today.

5 How would your church look different if every member loved others as freely as Jesus did? How would your community look different if everyone loved others in this way? How would the world look different?

Wednesday 2 March

1 Have you ever walked a labyrinth? What did God reveal to you while you walked? What other walking journeys have helped you to grow spiritually?

2 As we enter the season of Lent, how are you encouraged by imagining Jesus walking with you? What does it mean to you to accept his yoke? How will travelling with Jesus in this way help you to walk lightly during Lent?

3 When you find that your path in life is not straight, are you frustrated or do you enjoy the twists and turns? What spiritual practices help you to find your way? How do you walk with God rather than journey to find God?

4 Where do you feel the Spirit leading you today? Is it a path you are comfortable taking, or does it make you apprehensive? What prayers and scripture passages bring you peace?

5 In what new ways will you seek God's guidance during Lent? Name specific ways you will slow down to listen for God and enjoy your journey in this season.

Wednesday 9 March

1 Where do you go for your private devotional time? Why do you choose this spot? How do you think location affects the quality or style of your time with God?

2 How do you feel when you know that others are praying for you? Do you notice a change in your mindset or your situation when you know someone is praying for you?

3 Do you have a specific prayer practice to help you pray for those around you? If so, describe it. If not, what reminds you to pray for others?

4 Who has had a positive influence on your life and faith? Why? In what ways do you now strive to be a positive influence in the lives of others?

5 Name some scripture verses that assure you that God hears and answers prayers. What about these verses comforts you?

Wednesday 16 March

1 Recall a time when you held on to an old habit or routine that no longer served you. What made you realise that it was time to let go of the habit or routine? What changes did you see in your life when you finally let it go?

2 How do you observe Lent? Do you give something up? Do you take on a new practice? How does observing Lent help you grow in your faith?

3   Describe a time when you gained a new perspective on a familiar scripture passage. How does praying and discussing scripture with other Christians change the way you see certain parts of the Bible?

4   When God guides you in a new direction, are you happy to follow? Why or why not? How do you respond when you do not want to go where God guides you?

5   In what ways do others encourage you to let go of the old and to embrace the new? How do you encourage others to do this? Discuss the importance of helping one another in this way.

Wednesday 23 March

1   Where do you go for rest and relaxation? What do you find relaxing about this location? Name a lesson you have learned while in this place.

2   Do you find that nature teaches you lessons about yourself or your faith? Why or why not? How do you remain open to the lessons God has for you each day?

3   What role do more mature believers play in your faith journey? How has their role changed over time? How do you strive to help new believers now?

4   What does it mean to you to 'take flight' in your faith journey? What does it look like to stay close to the nest? Who in your faith community most encourages you to take flight?

5   Where do you find courage and joy in sharing your faith with others? How do you know when to share your faith? In what ways do you strive to be like Jesus as you witness to others?

Wednesday 30 March

1   Today's writer reminds us that God has a season for every plant to be beautiful. In what ways does this encourage you?

2 When you are going through a difficult time, what do you showcase? How do you strive to showcase God's presence and strength when you are going through hard times?

3 How does changing your perspective help you to feel more positive about your situation? What scripture passages help you to focus on God in all circumstances?

4 Where do you feel God's Spirit reviving you right now? How does being renewed by God help us to better share God's love with others?

5 In scripture, who found strength by focusing on the Lord? What can you learn from these examples?

Wednesday 6 April

1 What does it feel like to hear the words you are forgiven? What does it feel like to say those words to someone? Why do you think there is so much power in forgiveness?

2 Do you find it easier to hold on to guilt and regret or to confess and ask for forgiveness? Why? How does confessing and letting go of your sins change your situation?

3 How do the many examples of Jesus' offering forgiveness to people – even up to the moment of his death – affect the way you forgive others? What do these examples teach you about forgiveness and the way God forgives us?

4 In what ways are you comforted knowing that God always forgives us? Does that security make it easier for you to confess your sins to God? Why or why not?

5 Whom do you need to forgive today? Whose forgiveness do you seek today? What prayers and scripture passages give you courage and strength to confess and to forgive?

Wednesday 13 April

1 The writer of today's meditation talks about target fixation. In addition to our focus on God, name some ways that this can apply to the spiritual life.

2 When you are faced with a challenge, do you tend to focus on the problem or to look ahead? Why? How does this affect the outcome of your situation?

3 Who in your life helps to guide you through the obstacles you encounter? In what ways do they help you? How has their influence improved your life?

4 Which of God's promises brings you the most hope and peace right now? Why? What spiritual practices help you to keep that promise of God in focus every day?

5 How does spending time in community with other Christians help you to refocus on God's presence and promises? What differences do you notice in your mindset when you are unable to spend time with your faith community?

Wednesday 20 April

1 Are you close with people who do not share your faith? What is that relationship like? When do your faith differences seem like a challenge?

2 In what ways do you strive to witness to others through your words and actions? Do you find that your actions often make a bigger impact than your words when witnessing to others? How does that change the way you witness?

3 What does it look like for you to make the most of every opportunity to share your faith? How are you careful about the way you witness to those around you?

4   How do you respond when your efforts to witness to someone do not bear the fruit you hoped? What scripture verses encourage you to keep witnessing? In what ways do you see God working in the lives of those to whom you witness?

5   Who has been the greatest Christian witness to you? What did they do that made such a difference in your life?

Wednesday 27 April

1   Have you ever experienced division or a split among a group of believers? If so, what was that experience like? Describe the situation. How was the division resolved?

2   Why do you think Christian communities sometimes fall apart? What do you think helps keep them together? How does your faith community deal with internal disagreements?

3   Why is it so easy to attend to our own desires and to 'hurry off to our own houses'? What is there about focusing on our own desires that makes building community difficult?

4   Name some ways that you help to foster faithful community. How do these things nourish your faith? In what new ways would you like to start fostering community?

5   Name some ways your church works to create peace and unity in the congregation. How could your church improve? What can you do to support those improvements?

Journal page

Journal page

Journal page

Journal page

Become a Friend of BRF
and give regularly
to support our ministry

We help people of all ages to grow in faith

We encourage and support individual Christians and churches as they serve and resource the changing spiritual needs of communities today.

Through **Anna Chaplaincy** we're enabling churches to provide spiritual care to older people

Through **Living Faith** we're nurturing faith and resourcing life-long discipleship

Through **Messy Church** we're helping churches to reach out to families

Through **Parenting for Faith** we're supporting parents as they raise their children in the Christian faith

Our ministry is only possible because of the generous support of individuals, churches, trusts and gifts in wills.

As we look to the future and make plans, **regular donations make a huge difference** in ensuring we can both start and finish projects well.

By becoming a Friend of BRF and giving regularly to our ministry you are partnering with us in the gospel and helping change lives.

How your gift makes a difference

£2 a month — Helps us to develop **Living Faith** resources to use in care homes and communities

£10 a month — Helps us to support churches running the **Parenting for Faith** course and stand alongside parents

£5 a month — Helps us to support **Messy Church** volunteers and resource and grow the wider network

£20 a month — Helps us to resource **Anna Chaplaincy** and improve spiritual care for older people

 # How to become a Friend of BRF

Set up a Direct Debit donation at **brf.org.uk/donate** or find out how to set up a Standing Order at **brf.org.uk/friends**

Contact the fundraising team

Email: **giving@brf.org.uk**
Tel: +44 (0)1235 462305
Post: Fundraising team, BRF, 15 The Chambers, Vineyard, Abingdon OX14 3FE

Good to know

If you have any questions, or if you want to change your regular donation or stop giving in the future, do get in touch.

Registered with

FR

FUNDRAISING **REGULATOR**

SHARING OUR VISION – MAKING A ONE-OFF GIFT

I would like to make a donation to support BRF.
Please use my gift for:

☐ Where it is most needed ☐ Anna Chaplaincy ☐ Living Faith

☐ Messy Church ☐ Parenting for Faith

Title	First name/initials	Surname

Address

	Postcode

Email

Telephone

Signature	Date

Our ministry is only possible because of the generous support of individuals, churches, trusts and gifts in wills.

giftaid it You can add an extra 25p to every £1 you give.

Please treat as Gift Aid donations all qualifying gifts of money made

☐ today, ☐ in the past four years, ☐ and in the future.

I am a UK taxpayer and understand that if I pay less Income Tax and/or Capital Gains Tax in the current tax year than the amount of Gift Aid claimed on all my donations, it is my responsibility to pay any difference.

☐ My donation does not qualify for Gift Aid.

Please notify BRF if you want to cancel this Gift Aid declaration, change your name or home address, or no longer pay sufficient tax on your income and/or capital gains.

Please complete other side of form

SHARING OUR VISION – MAKING A ONE-OFF GIFT

Please accept my gift of:

☐ £2 ☐ £5 ☐ £10 ☐ £20 Other £ _____

by (*delete as appropriate*):

☐ Cheque/Charity Voucher payable to 'BRF'

☐ MasterCard/Visa/Debit card/Charity card

Name on card _____

Card no. ☐☐☐☐ ☐☐☐☐ ☐☐☐☐ ☐☐☐☐

Expires end ☐☐ ☐☐   Security code ☐☐☐   Last 3 digits on the reverse of the card

Signature _____   Date _____

☐ I would like to leave a gift to BRF in my will.
Please send me further information.

For help or advice regarding making a gift, please contact our fundraising team +44 (0)1865 462305

Your privacy

We will use your personal data to process this transaction. From time to time we may send you information about the work of BRF that we think may be of interest to you. Our privacy policy is available at **brf.org.uk/privacy**. Please contact us if you wish to discuss your mailing preferences.

Registered with

FUNDRAISING **REGULATOR**

↶ Please complete other side of form

Please return this form to 'Freepost BRF'
No other address information or stamp is needed

Bible Reading Fellowship is a charity (233280) and company limited by guarantee (301324), registered in England and Wales

UR0122

What is the Easter story really about, and how do we share it? Through each week of Lent, Sally Welch examines a different aspect of the Easter story: *repenting*, *changing*, *hoping*, *trusting*, *forgiving*, *loving* and *sacrificing*. Within each week, the days are focused on what we need to do in order to share the story: *listening*, *understanding*, *reflecting*, *living*, *telling*, *sharing* and *becoming*. Each day offers a Bible passage, followed by a reflection and prayer activity. Suggestions for group study questions are also included.

Sharing the Easter Story
From reading to living the gospel
Sally Welch
978 1 80039 098 0 £8.99
brfonline.org.uk

Some women of the Hebrew scriptures are well known, but many others are barely remembered. Even when they are, we often don't pause on them long enough to think about what we might learn from them. *Unveiled*, written with frankness and humour and illustrated with striking artwork from a young Oxford-based artist, explores the stories of 40 women in 40 days. Each reflection ends with a short application to everyday life, guidance for further thought and a prayer.

Unveiled
Women of the Old Testament and the choices they made
Reflections by Clare Hayns; artwork by Micah Hayns
978 1 80039 072 0 £12.99
brfonline.org.uk

How to encourage Bible reading in your church

BRF has been helping individuals connect with the Bible for over 90 years. We want to support churches as they seek to encourage church members into regular Bible reading.

Order a Bible reading resources pack

This pack is designed to give your church the tools to publicise our Bible reading notes. It includes:

- Sample Bible reading notes for your congregation to try.
- Publicity resources, including a poster.
- A church magazine feature about Bible reading notes.

The pack is free, but we welcome a £5 donation to cover the cost of postage. If you require a pack to be sent outside the UK or require a specific number of sample Bible reading notes, please contact us for postage costs. More information about what the current pack contains is available on our website.

How to order and find out more

- Visit **biblereadingnotes.org.uk/for-churches**.
- Telephone BRF on +44 (0)1865 319700 Mon–Fri 9.30–17.00.
- Write to us at BRF, 15 The Chambers, Vineyard, Abingdon OX14 3FE.

Keep informed about our latest initiatives

We are continuing to develop resources to help churches encourage people into regular Bible reading, wherever they are on their journey. Join our email list at **brfonline.org.uk/signup** to stay informed about the latest initiatives that your church could benefit from.

Subscriptions

The Upper Room is published in January, May and September.

Individual subscriptions
The subscription rate for orders for 4 or fewer copies includes postage and packing:

The Upper Room annual individual subscription   £18.30

Group subscriptions
Orders for 5 copies or more, sent to ONE address, are post free:
The Upper Room annual group subscription   £14.55

Please do not send payment with order for a group subscription. We will send an invoice with your first order.

Please note that the annual billing period for group subscriptions runs from 1 May to 30 April.

Copies of the notes may also be obtained from Christian bookshops.

Single copies of *The Upper Room* cost £4.85.

Prices valid until 30 April 2023.

Giant print version
The Upper Room is available in giant print for the visually impaired, from:

Torch Trust for the Blind
Torch House
Torch Way
Northampton Road
Market Harborough
LE16 9HL

Tel: +44 (0)1858 438260
torchtrust.org

**All our Bible reading notes can be ordered online by visiting
brfonline.org.uk/subscriptions**

☐ I would like to take out a subscription myself (complete your name
and address details once)

☐ I would like to give a gift subscription (please provide both names
and addresses)

Title .... First name/initials .... Surname ....

Address ....

.... Postcode ....

Telephone .... Email ....

Gift subscription name ....

Gift subscription address ....

.... Postcode ....

Gift message (20 words max. or include your own gift card):

....

....

Please send **The Upper Room** beginning with the May 2022 /
September 2022 / January 2023 issue (*delete as appropriate*):

Annual individual subscription ☐ £18.30

Optional donation* to support the work of BRF £ ....

Total enclosed £ .... (cheques should be made payable to 'BRF')

*Please complete and return the Gift Aid declaration on page 159 to make your
  donation even more valuable to us.

Method of payment

Please charge my MasterCard / Visa with £ ....

Card no. ☐☐☐☐ ☐☐☐☐ ☐☐☐☐ ☐☐☐☐

Expires end ☐☐ ☐☐ Security code ☐☐☐ Last 3 digits on the
reverse of the card

All our Bible reading notes can be ordered online by visiting brfonline.org.uk/subscriptions

☐ Please send me .... copies of *The Upper Room* May 2022 / September 2022 / January 2023 issue (*delete as appropriate*)

Title .... First name/initials .... Surname ....

Address ....

.... Postcode ....

Telephone .... Email ....

Please do not send payment with this order. We will send an invoice with your first order.

Christian bookshops: All good Christian bookshops stock BRF publications. For your nearest stockist, please contact BRF.

Telephone: The BRF office is open Mon–Fri 9.30–17.00. To place your order, telephone +44 (0)1865 319700.

Online: brfonline.org.uk/group-subscriptions

☐ Please send me a Bible reading resources pack to encourage Bible reading in my church

Please return this form with the appropriate payment to:
BRF, 15 The Chambers, Vineyard, Abingdon OX14 3FE

For terms and cancellation information, please visit **brfonline.org.uk/terms**.

Bible Reading Fellowship is a charity (233280) and company limited by guarantee (301324), registered in England and Wales

UR0122

To order

Online: **brfonline.org.uk**
Telephone: +44 (0)1865 319700 Mon–Fri 9.30–17.00

Delivery times within the UK are normally 15 working days. Prices are correct at the time of going to press but may change without prior notice.

Title	Price	Qty	Total
Sharing the Easter Story (BRF Lent Book 2022)	£8.99		
Unveiled	£12.99		

POSTAGE AND PACKING CHARGES			
Order value	UK	Europe	Rest of world
Under £7.00	£2.00	Available on request	Available on request
£7.00–£29.99	£3.00		
£30.00 and over	FREE		

Total value of books	
Postage and packing	
Donation*	
Total for this order	

* Please complete the Gift Aid declaration below

Please complete in BLOCK CAPITALS

Title .... First name/initials .... Surname...

Address ....

.... Postcode ....

Acc. No. .... Telephone ....

Email ....

Gift Aid Declaration

gift aid it

Please treat as Gift Aid donations all qualifying gifts of money made

☐ today, ☐ in the past four years, ☐ and in the future **or** ☐ My donation does not qualify for Gift Aid.

I am a UK taxpayer and understand that if I pay less Income Tax and/or Capital Gains Tax in the current tax year than the amount of Gift Aid claimed on all my donations, it is my responsibility to pay any difference.

Please notify BRF if you want to cancel this declaration, change your name or home address, or no longer pay sufficient tax on your income and/or capital gains.

Method of payment

☐ Cheque (made payable to BRF) ☐ MasterCard / Visa

Card no. ☐☐☐☐ ☐☐☐☐ ☐☐☐☐ ☐☐☐☐

Expires end ☐☐ ☐☐ Security code ☐☐☐ Last 3 digits on the reverse of the card

Please return this form to:

BRF, 15 The Chambers, Vineyard, Abingdon OX14 3FE | **enquiries@brf.org.uk**

For terms and cancellation information, please visit **brfonline.org.uk/terms**.

Bible Reading Fellowship is a charity (233280) and company limited by guarantee (301324), registered in England and Wales

Enabling all ages to grow in faith

Anna Chaplaincy
Living Faith
Messy Church
Parenting for Faith

100 years of BRF

2022 is BRF's 100th anniversary! Look out for details of our special new centenary resources, a beautiful centenary rose and an online thanksgiving service that we hope you'll attend. This centenary year we're focusing on sharing the story of BRF, the story of the Bible – and we hope you'll share your stories of faith with us too.

Find out more at **brf.org.uk/centenary**.

To find out more about our work, visit
brf.org.uk

Sharing
the Story
since 1922